STUDIES IN THE U

Privatization
and the
public sector

Bryan Hurl
Head of Economics
at Harrow School

HEINEMANN
EDUCATIONAL

For Geraldine

Heinemann Educational Books Ltd
Halley Court, Jordan Hill, Oxford OX2 8EJ

OXFORD   LONDON   EDINBURGH
MELBOURNE   SYDNEY   AUCKLAND
SINGAPORE   MADRID   IBADAN
NAIROBI   GABORONE   HARARE
KINGSTON   PORTSMOUTH NH

First published 1988

British Library Cataloguing in Publication Data
Hurl, Bryan
    Privatization and the public sector.
    (Studies in the UK economy).
    1. Great Britain. Public sector.
    Privatization
    I. Title   II. Series
    354.4107'2

ISBN 0 435 33003 9

Typeset by Fakenham Photosetting Ltd., Fakenham, Norfolk
Printed and bound in Great Britain by Biddles Ltd, Guildford, Surrey

Acknowledgements

To 'Lyn Darley who retyped the manuscript countless times to cope with my many, semi-legible alterations.

To M.E.S. for acting as a sounding board for my 'silly' ideas.

To Rosalind Levačić for constructive criticism.

To Michael and 'Stin for creative hospitality in Tuscany.

Thanks are also due to the following for permission to reproduce copyright material: *Financial Times* for the articles on pp. 7–8 and 74; The Controller of Her Majesty's Stationery Office for the diagram on p. 10, the graphs on pp. 29, 30, 37, 85 and the tables on pp. 33–4; *Independent* for the article on p. 67; Mail Newspapers plc for the article on p. 35; *Observer* for the article on p. 50; Royal Bank of Scotland for the table on p. 48; *The Times* for the articles on pp. 41–2, 63, 66–7 and 90–91; Richard Willson for the cartoons on pp. 5 and 31.

Contents

Preface

My teaching of A-level and AS-level Economics has thrown up two significant problems:

- Although good textbooks make much of the importance of the *public sector*, they then fail to do it justice.
- The march of *privatization* has been so rapid that the subject is absent from most textbooks.

It seemed reasonable, therefore, to try to combine the two topics into a booklet. It is one of a new series of topical booklets designed to be up to date and fill gaps in the standard texts.

Subsequently, restrained by the quota of pages thought desirable for a text at the right price, I have, of course, had to compromise. So I have sought instead to interrelate the two topics where this is possible. The aim is to equip the student reader with sufficient expertise to be able to discourse meaningfully on the economics of the public sector in general and the economics of privatization in particular.

I follow the profession's norm of making an assumption: readers have been taught their basic grammar – microeconomics – but may not have moved on to macroeconomics.

As I find economics intrinsically interesting and so many texts on it staggeringly dull ('dismal', Mr Carlyle, I agree), I have sought to communicate my excitement by showing this subject to be an up-to-the-minute activity to be evaluated as it takes place. Any constructive ideas from teacher or taught on how to improve on this first attempt will be warmly acknowledged. In the oligopolistic market for economics texts, the non-price competition of research and development, to improve quality, is to be welcomed as a welfare gain for the consumer!

B.H.

Chapter One
Privatization in the 1980s

'Selling off the family silver . . .' Lord Stockton

Privatization has taken the world by storm and it has taken it by surprise. Well-publicized are the aims of the Russian leader, Mikhail Gorbachev, who wants to reduce the role of *Gosplan* in allocating resources in the command economy of the USSR to allow some enterprises to plan inputs and outputs according to market forces. All round the world – in France, Germany, Canada, Mexico, Argentina, Ghana, Mozambique, Japan, Australia, New Zealand and ninety other countries – privatization schemes are being actively pursued.

The surprise in Britain – the world's leading privatization country – is that the Conservative Party's election manifesto of 1979, which was supposed to offer to the electorate its 'menu' of choice at the polls, failed to mention the word. Nearly a decade later, as the 1980s move to a close, a major transformation has been started on the British economy and the world's biggest asset sale – that of electricity – is about to be floated. The programme shows signs of having been adopted by accident rather than by design.

This programme in Britain has taken economics by surprise too. Give your textbook the *privatization test*: check to see if the topic is covered at all. If it is, is it done thoroughly, or does it look suspiciously as if an older book has been updated with a few added paragraphs?

My pupils, in the 1970s, passed A-level Economics ignorant of the word. It was certainly not in their textbooks. Not until 1983 did a well-respected dictionary of economics, much used in schools (see page 4), add to its third edition a definition along the following lines:

Privatization: The sale of government-owned equity in nationalized industries or other commercial enterprises, to private investors, with or without the loss of government control of the organizations.

This would have been recognized by my pupils as a definition of **denationalization** whereby the government sold its **equity** – its notional shares as the owner of a public sector enterprise – so that shares could again be quoted and bought and sold on the stock market.

The *steel industry* was a political shuttlecock that was used in the

1

Table 1 Proceeds from the 'sale of silver' (HM Treasury figures)*

Company	Date begun†	Proceeds (£m)
British Petroleum	1979	276
National Enterprise Board Holdings	1979	122
British Aerospace	1981	389
North Sea Licences	1981	349
British Sugar Corporation	1981	44
Cable & Wireless	1981	1 024
Amersham International	1982	64
National Freight Corporation‡	1982	5
Britoil	1982	1 053
Associated British Ports	1983	97
International Aeradio	1983	60
British Telecom	1984	3 682
BT loan stock	1984	158
Enterprise Oil	1984	382
British Gas	1986	5 090
British Gas Debt	1986	750
BT preference shares	1986	250
British Airways	1987	825
Royal Ordnance	1987	190
Rolls Royce	1987	1 360
BAA	1987	1 250
British Petroleum	1987	1 100
Miscellaneous	1979–88	527
Total		19 029

* The table is based on a narrow definition of privatization (i.e. asset sales of central government the proceeds of which were paid to HM Treasury after a public flotation). Refer to pages 70–72 for a wider definition of privatization.
† Some sales were paid for in instalments over more than a year.
‡ The NFC was a management/worker private flotation.

knockabout game played between Labour and Conservative governments: it was nationalized, denationalized and renationalized. At the time of writing (1988) the steel industry has been brought forward to the front of the queue for ... denationalization? or privatization? Is there a difference?

My own definition of privatization is shown in Figure 1. We shall need to analyse this definition in more detail in Chapter 4. As privatization proceeds the legal experts who work for **merchant banks** (which the government uses to float the new issues of shares) invent new legal variations on the general theme. Cross Channel Hovercraft would slip

---

Denationalization the sale of public sector assets

As well as nationalized industries this also includes companies and local authority council houses. Table 1 summarizes the sales so far by the UK Treasury. It omits the proceeds from council house sales which go directly to the councils concerned.

Deregulation (a synonym is *liberalization*) the removal of legal barriers to entry to a previously protected market to allow private enterprise to compete

Public sector provision (financing) and public sector production are replaced by private provision and production. An example is bus services.

Franchising the public sector continues financial provision but for private sector production

This was pioneered by Southend Council in 1980. Many councils have now contracted out refuse collection, street cleaning and meals and laundry services in hospitals.

Figure 1 My three-point definition of *privatization*

through the net unless it is pointed out that the government gave it away....

So my classic quotation from Lord Stockton begins to look less than accurate: it is hardly appropriate for **deregulation** or **franchising**. But it has become a cliché of the critics of Margaret Thatcher's privatizing governments of the 1980s. They have accused her of *selling the family silver to subsidize a riotous living,* claiming that, rather than raise taxes or cut public expenditure, her governments have sought to gain revenue for income tax cuts from what Neil Kinnock calls *the privatization swag.*

What is the economic truth of this supposed irresponsible prodigality? A full answer will have to wait until Chapter 6, but it is worth complimenting the phrase in the quotation as a piece of political rhetoric. Selling the silver is dire – but as economics the phrase is less than satisfactory.

If you sell off your family silver to spend on an irresponsible spree you very obviously lose the silver. If, however, the state sells off 'our' silver

3

we do not lose it – it stays in the family because we are all part of the same family. If you used nationalized gas and telephones before privatization then you now use them still – from British Gas plc and British Telecom plc. Neither the gas nor the telephone systems have disappeared.

It would be much more appropriate to discuss the merits or otherwise of redistributing the family silver amidst a greater number of the family, since this has produced economic changes of great importance. The proceeds of privatization have benefited particular groups and there may be conflicts of interest. The merchant banks employed by the government to float and underwrite the issues had, until the British Petroleum flop in 1987, made huge profits along with the related institutions that worked on these over-publicized flotations. These institutions have been very happy to take their part of the 'swag'. Selling deliberately under-priced shares has created a new breed of stock market gambler and source of capital gain income. Shares oversubscribed ten, twenty or thirty times sounds more like the Roaring Twenties and the world of Scott Fitzgerald. Equity is a vital concept in economic theory: there will be more to say on this subject in Chapter 5. It should not be confused with *share equity* but understood to involve *fairness*.

If a dictionary can offer a less than perfect definition of privatization – and a famous politician a misunderstanding about the issue – this might imply that the topic is a difficult one. Actually the topic is far from difficult; we just need to scrutinize the public sector in theory and in practice (as we do here in Chapters 2 and 3), because it is the claimed disadvantages of the public sector provision of goods and services which generate the arguments in favour of privatization. In which case, an examination then of privatization in theory and in practice (Chapters 4 and 5) will allow us to weigh the economic evidence for the conclusion, in Chapter 6, of the consequences of privatization for the public sector.

• *A simple research task*   On page 1 you saw a definition of privatization derived from a much-used dictionary. The publication was, in fact, the Penguin Dictionary of Economics, edited by Bannock, Baxter and Rees. Now check the fourth edition (published in 1987) for its updated definition. What has been added to this edition to improve the definition already quoted? Is the definition now satisfactory (i.e. comprehensive enough)?

KEY WORDS

Command economy   Merchant banks
Denationalization   Deregulation
Equity   Franchising

Reading list

Kay, Mayer and Thompson, Introduction in *Privatization and Regulation*, Clarendon Press, 1986, pp. 1–32.

Smith, D., Introduction in *Mrs Thatcher's Economics*, Heinemann Educational Books, 1988.

The Economist, 'Selling the silver' in *Britain's Business*, Economist Newspapers Ltd, 1986, pp. 6–7.

Wiltshire, K., Chapter One of *Privatisation, the British Experience*, Longman Cheshire, 1987.

The Secretary of State for Trade and Industry lifts the hammer to finalize the sale of another piece of family silver, Lot 10, the Rover Group, being held in front of the buyers by its Chairman. This cartoon is reprinted by kind permission of the artist, Richard Willson.

Data response question 1
The consumer is the loser

This exercise is designed to give you some background on issues to which we shall have to address ourselves. It may be that an economist's view will differ from what you read in the accompanying newspaper article written by John Edmonds of the General, Municipal and Boilermakers Union (published in the *Financial Times*, 16 September 1987). Even so, Mr Edmonds poses a relevant question in his penultimate paragraph: *Which structures and relationships best deliver the goods and services to the public?*

Now answer the following questions.

1. How many of the three forms of privatization defined in Figure 1 are mentioned by name?
2. Is this a normative or positive study of privatization? Use a quotation to substantiate your answer.
3. What is the function of a trade union?
4. What are the explicit anxieties of the writer over the treatment of trade unionists in privatized firms?
5. What does the writer think the motivation of worker shareholders adds up to?
6. What constructive responses can a union make to a privatization proposal?
7. What is a regulatory agency? Name some regulatory agents in your school.
8. Has privatization broken up monopolies in gas and telephones? Will it in electricity and water?
9. Why is the consumer the loser?

Consumer is the loser

SINCE 1979, privatisation has travelled from the far reaches of the UK Conservative Party's right wing fringe to the centre stage of the present Government's 1987 election manifesto and subsequent legislative programme.

In turn, the one commonplace, defensive trade union reaction of concentrating solely on jobs and defending the status quo in services, regardless of deficiencies, has itself had to go.

The trade unions' initial view was that the policy was so self-evidently foolish that no government would get away with it. Next came strident campaigns of opposition and then a feeling of some alarm at our apparent lack of public support.

The early campaigns were difficult to mount because the Government's policy changed rapidly. Initially conceived as a mechanism for deregulation, increased competition and anti-statism, privatisation has since become an indispensable revenue raiser for a Government whose commitments – to reduced income tax rates, lower public borrowing and macroeconomic policies that leave a substantial social security bill to be picked up as the price for mass unemployment – cannot otherwise be reconciled.

When in 1984 the Government's forward plans for public expenditure revealed that asset sales of £14bn-plus were needed over three years to balance the books, privatisation was firmly established as a mechanism for raising revenue rather than as a policy for promoting competition by breaking up monopolies and other large units.

So British Telecom and British Gas were not opened up to greater competition. Public monopolies became private monopolies and the Treasury took the spoils. It will be the same with water and electricity: the demands of the Treasury will take priority over the libertarian inclinations of Conservative theoreticians.

The situation is further confused by an official ambivalence as to whether privatisation as a labour market policy is supposed to be a pleasurable experience – the "carrot" of lucrative worker shareholdings and more liberal promotion structures – or a stern discipline for a "lax" public sector.

In fact, 250,000 members of my union in the public services, are now faced with the possibility of their jobs being contracted-out to operators who have an appalling record as employers.

The instances of poor service provision – filthy hospital wards, squalid kitchens and uncleaned schools – where contractors have moved in, are matched by cases of arbitrary treatment of staff, of enforced reductions in hours, and thus in pay, and the stripping away of basic conditions in terms of holiday entitlement and sick pay provisions.

Even in those enterprises which have been privatised by share flotation, the significance of worker shareholdings is in danger of being overstated to the point of absurdity. As a way of involving a workforce in decisions and therefore in the fortunes of an enterprise its significance is just about zero. So if contracting out has been bad news for the workers affected, and if flotation has been largely an irrelevance for workers in former public industries, can it all be justified in terms of benefits for consumers? The only clear message seems to be that privatisation has exploded the myth of a free market dealing in an even-handed way with undifferentiated consumers.

Some consumers are clearly more equal than others, as millions of domestic telephone users and millions more gas consumers will testify. The removal or downgrading of public service conditions in the operations of privatised businesses has brought about a significant shift in the priority groups which the new companies have sought to serve.

Privatisation has made the interests of the consumers of services (and of those who work in providing them) subservient to the often short-term interests of investors – and especially the large institutional investors – on whom the Government depends for the revenue raising exercise that privatisation has become.

And it is an argument that is reverberating noisily in the case of the water industry at present in the form of a debate about the powers to be given to the regulatory agencies *vis-à-vis* those of the water authorities.

When proposals for the disposal of the nuclear industry take firmer shape the arguments about public responsibilities of private operators will become even more acute.

It is not surprising, then, that the most significant development in the trade union response to privatisation has been the establishment of strong links with those who represent the consumers of public services which are now on the Government's shopping list.

In the water industry, for example, a wide alliance has been built up between those who work in the water authorities, environmentalists and leisure groups who use the industry's facilities.The same approach is governing our response to privatisation plans for the electricity industry and the proposals for compulsory tendering for local authority services.

To that extent, privatisation has posed an important challenge to unions, as to the Left in politics. The challenge is to move away from rather sterile arguments about the pattern of ownership in industry and to concentrate instead on the much more practical question of which structures and relationships best deliver the goods and services to the public.

The irony is that the Government, by reducing its interest to a cash-raising one, has removed itself from this debate. It is now the unions which through the dialogue which has been opened with users of services, are taking that debate forward.

Chapter Two

The public sector in theory

'... it is true that the Beveridge Report is signed by one man only –
myself – so that I am the only person that can be hanged for it.'
W. Beveridge

Preliminaries

In output terms the **public sector** includes *both* (i) the current output of
goods and services and the investment in new capital by central government and the local authorities (i.e. general government), *and* (ii) new
capital investment by the nationalized industries and their current
output of goods and services.

The proportion of the economy's annual **gross domestic product** –
GDP, the total of all goods and services – that general government
expenditure creates *directly* is approximately 25 per cent. A figure of
this size emphasizes the importance to the economy of the resources
used and why economists must study them.

A general trend in all the OECD countries (the richest 24 non-
communist nations) has been for public expenditure to rise. One reason
for this is the **relative price effect** – productivity grows only slowly in
government services compared with private industry, which has scope
for economies of scale, while the prices of government services rise
relative to those of the rest of the economy.

In the United Kingdom the struggles of the Conservative government
to contain public expenditure feature regularly. The government came
to power determined to cut this expenditure back in real terms in order
to reduce the burden of taxation that funds it. Meanwhile the Opposition calls for an *increase* in public expenditure. Caught in the crossfire is
privatization: if the government sells public sector assets it raises revenue *and* reduces the size of the public sector simultaneously.

In expenditure terms public expenditure is inflated to a bigger figure.
By adding **transfer payments** which households receive and subsidies to
firms, the figure rises to 42 per cent of the GDP. The decision-takers
who spend these sums are the recipients, not the government. Bear this
distinction in mind as we categorize public expenditure.

Figure 2 demonstrates how public expenditure can be studied in two

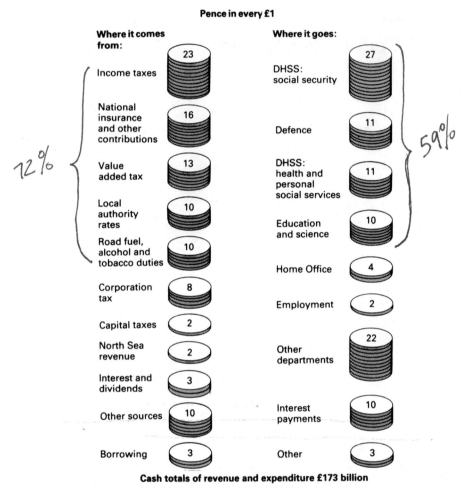

Pence in every £1

Where it comes from:

Income taxes	23
National insurance and other contributions	16
Value added tax	13
Local authority rates	10
Road fuel, alcohol and tobacco duties	10
Corporation tax	8
Capital taxes	2
North Sea revenue	2
Interest and dividends	3
Other sources	10
Borrowing	3

72%

Where it goes:

DHSS: social security	27
Defence	11
DHSS: health and personal social services	11
Education and science	10
Home Office	4
Employment	2
Other departments	22
Interest payments	10
Other	3

59%

Cash totals of revenue and expenditure £173 billion

Figure 2 Public money 1987–88 (reprinted from the Treasury's *EPR Supplement*, March/April 1987)

ways. If we look at it *functionally* (i.e. what the money is spent on) we see that 27 per cent of the total is for social security transfer payments to the sick, unemployed or old. This is top of the list at 27p in 'Where it goes'. The top five sources of tax revenue in 'Where it comes from' are income tax, national insurance poll tax on workers, VAT on expenditure, rates on property (soon to be replaced by the Community Charge), and duties on petrol, alcohol and tobacco. Together these raise what percentage of the total?

Alternatively we can look at the expenditure *economically* – what it is spent on in terms of an economist's categorization into public goods and merit goods.

A public good

This is a good or service that is difficult to price to an individual consumer. If it is to be provided for some it has to be provided for all. As it is impossible to prevent anybody from consuming it, so private capitalism is reluctant to supply it – it is *non-excludable* from the point of view of the seller. Public goods prevent a market system from generating an optimum allocation of resources.

A public good is an **externality**. The benefit people get depends not only on how much they have but also on how much other people have. The benefit each derives depends on how much of the good is in existence. Yet two individuals need not place the same value on marginal amounts because their marginal utilities differ. Public goods confer positive, benefiting externalities.

Public 'bads' confer negative externalities, which include polluted air, crime and poverty. A government, through legislation, can create a clean air zone and so change a public bad into a public good. Public expenditure on a judiciary and the police force reduces crime.

Additionally, a public good is *non-rival*. When household A consumes it this does not stop household B consuming it, simultaneously. On the other hand the typewriter that is printing this sentence was purchased in a market, at a price; it is a normal good which is both *excludable* and *rival*. It was provided by a firm which aimed to make a profit, to one buyer whose consumption of it prevented others buying it.

If you are a future entrepreneur you should reflect, for a moment, on whether you could build a lighthouse near dangerous rocks and charge passing mariners for the service you offer them. How would you prevent 'free riders', consumers unwilling to pay because payment is so easily avoidable?

A colleague of mine is an energetic member of the CND movement and on occasions we have had spirited disagreements at the lunch table. Defence is one of the rare examples of a pure public good, and the nuclear deterrent – which I want and he does not – is only available collectively. My colleague cannot opt out as an individual; collectively we have it or collectively we do not. Those who regard such as a disbenefit are 'reluctant riders'.

It is rare to find a pure public good. Because of congestion both roads and police can be partly rivalrous in consumption. Most examples are **impure public goods**: they have a private goods element. It is not part of the definition of a public good that it be publicly provided. While it is impossible to use a market system for most roads it is more than feasible to privatize the Severn Bridge and the Dartford Tunnel because they *are* excludable – the continental members of the EEC are great believers in motorway tolls. The television duopoly of the BBC and ITV provides non-excludable broadcasting. The BBC is in the public sector, funded by a licence fee due from all set owners. Commercial sponsors provide ITV, so a public good is in the private sector. It would be possible to privatize the BBC. Furthermore, with the deregulation of broadcasting, planned for 1992, cable television will further muddy the economists' classifications: cable TV will be metered to the individual user so this form of broadcasting will be a private good that is excludable....

Merit goods

These are goods which some people think others should consume more of. They are rival goods, and they are excludable. They confer direct benefits as well as external benefits.

A market for them could exist, private enterprise could offer them at a price, but insufficient would be consumed according to some social judgement. The **welfare state** provides NHS prescriptions at a nominal market price and schools and hospitals at no market price. A cherished belief of social reformers is that households would under-provide for themselves, in a market. For the low-paid, paying monthly health insurance premiums could be prohibitive.

Note the direct conflict with the economist's assumption that households are rational utility-maximizers, the arbiters of their own consumption. Laws against the consumption of heroin and glue sniffing call this into question. Compulsory seat-belt wearing saves lives. The state becomes paternalistic – it takes on the role of father-figure to decide for you, it becomes the Universal Provider State, it provides social security, i.e. sick pay, unemployment benefit, pensions, health care, housing and education. Unfortunately this means that the state becomes a near monopoly provider of these services, because there is limited competition from private hospitals and fee-paying independent schools. Ninety-three per cent of children consume state education for which there is no market charge. Reflect for a moment on how your school fits into economic theory:

- Is it a firm?
- Does it need factors of production?
- What is its output?
- How efficient is it?

If your parents had to pay for you to attend school would they buy the best at a price or go for a cheaper one so that a better car and frequent continental holidays could also be consumed by your household? Incidentally the externality you are deriving from being educated includes making you a better citizen, so do you agree that education can be classified also as an impure public good?

The architect of the welfare state, Lord Beveridge, created a universal provider state available to all. He was most certainly not hanged for it. Forty years on governments have started to look more critically at how to restrain the public sector expenditure groups, to question whether resources are being used effectively and to ask what the priorities should be if the GDP has too many claimants. Social security transfer payments for the sick, unemployed and retired and direct expenditure on doctors, nurses and hospitals and on teachers and schools, are three of the top four spenders according to Figure 2. Trying to reform the funding of the welfare state is an aspect of privatization in the 1980s which will require further study in later chapters.

Transfer payments

These help to swell the public sector percentage of the GDP. They are direct money transfers on the Robin Hood principle of redistribution of income, especially to two large groups, the *unemployed* and the *retired*. This is another fundamental part of the welfare state: giving cash to members of society whose skills are not required although they are a part of the labour force; or who are deemed too old to contribute their labour to the GDP. They are protected from being rational utility 'compromisers' – they could provide for these circumstances by voluntary saving and by buying insurance in a market, but would be likely to under-provide when young, healthy and working.

Public money

You are now in a position to make an economic study of the functional Figure 2. There is too much to memorize, but any good A-level candidate should know the statistics for the top four, double-digit, consumers of public expenditure on the right-hand side. Remember these four and their percentages. Remember, too, the top five sources of tax revenue, which I have mentioned already.

Notice the last entry on the left-hand side of the diagram. This could be used as further evidence that the family silver is being sold off to subsidize a riotous living. . . . There will be more to be said on this point later, in Chapter 6.

The economics of the mixed economy

In Britain's **mixed economy** some goods are provided by private capitalism in markets with a price mechanism and some are provided by central and local government in the non-market sector. The nationalized industries operate in the market sector but their assets are publicly owned; they merit a separate section shortly.

The economic argument for the mixed economy is that without government intervention there will be *market failure*, where public and merit goods will be under-provided. When the 'right' bundle of these is provided then *social benefits* are gained by society in general as well as by the individual consumer. These are externalities: public sector sewerage schemes remove epidemics, contagious diseases are reduced, the black death becomes of historical, rather than topical, interest. A state-educated workforce is more productive than an illiterate one.

Income redistribution, which Robin Hood practised illegally and the reformers initiated legally, is a mark of a caring society – unless it is brutally confiscatory in its methods.

Economics texts make much of the virtues of the price mechanism, as we shall see shortly, in evaluating privatization. But a defect is that **desired demand** is of no economic consequence in a market; only **effective demand**, backed up by purchasing power, qualifies. Adam Smith's oft-quoted 'invisible hand' does not acknowledge the price mechanism's inability to record compassion: it can produce mink coats for the rich but not children's shoes for paupers.

Unequal factor endowments produce, inevitably, unequal incomes and wealth in a capitalist society; were this society *laissez faire* – non-interventionist in the sense that the government withdraws from the provision of merit goods, transfer payments and subsidies – then the distribution of income could well become $L_1/L_2/L_3/L_4$ on the **Lorenz curve** (see Figure 3). This curve shows the relationship between the cumulative percentage of incomes and households such that, in a perfectly egalitarian society, 25 per cent of households at A would have 25 per cent of incomes; and at B, 50 per cent of them would have 50 per cent of incomes. We shall call this Erewhon (an anagram of Nowhere). A *laissez faire* society would have gross disparities, as at L_4 where the top 5 per cent are very rich with 75 per cent of income because 95 per cent of households have only 25 per cent.

A mixed economy with a prominent public sector shifts the curve to M_1, M_2 and M_3, using income taxes, wealth taxes, transfer payments and subsidies. Public sector goods and services provide part of a household's **standard of living**. Household X with two children at a state school, one of whom needs frequent NHS medical attention, has a

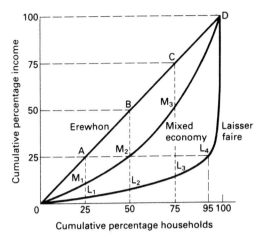

Figure 3 Lorenz curve

higher social wage (income in kind) than household Y, a bachelor schoolmaster with the same net money income. X consumes education and health; Y, who is fit and active, neither.

Privatization can change the distribution of incomes if firms prosper after their asset sales, and the distribution of wealth if those who buy the privatized shares find that their value rises. Table 5 on page 57 shows how silver has turned to gold.

The largest saleable assets are the **nationalized industries.**

Subsidized goods and services

These are provided in a market but their prices are not a true reflection of the cost of the factor inputs; they are lower because of grants to make them so. Sending a letter from London to a farmhouse in a remote Scottish glen costs a great deal more than its market price (its postage stamp). To finance it surplus revenue from other, profitable, postal deliveries is used as a cross-subsidy.

The government can subsidize both households and firms. The rent charged by a local authority for living in a council house is not determined by the market: it is a fraction of what a private landlord would charge. Cheap-rent council houses are part of the provision of the welfare state.

As part of the government's Regional Policy, firms in designated Development Areas, where unemployment is particularly high, qualify for cash grants to subsidize new factories and jobs.

When Rolls-Royce went bankrupt, the government took its assets into public ownership and subsidized further output and investment.

15

Some of the nationalized industries trade at a loss and require Exchequer grants for their deficit financing. Examples are coal, railways and ship building.

Merit goods are subsidized. Transfer payments are subsidies. Pure public goods are offered at zero price to all, regardless of different marginal benefits derived by individuals.

As a separate but overlapping category, 'subsidized goods' will henceforth be used to refer to private production in a market where the price mechanism, to the final consumer is used but where additional funding is available from the public purse, as shown in Figure 4.

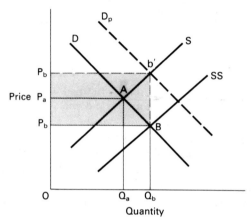

Figure 4 Cash subsidy to a firm

The demand for a given product is shown by the demand curve D. Without a subsidy the supply curve is S. If the government is prepared to pay a specific subsidy of £x per unit, then instead of a market-determined equilibrium at A, which gives a price P_a and a quantity demanded and supplied of Q_a, the firm, or nationalized industry, reacts by supplying a greater quantity Q_b. Because the subsidized price is reduced to P_b, demand expands to B from A. The firm receives two sources of income:

- From the consumer in the market, the price times quantity is represented by the rectangle OP_bBQ_b.
- From the taxpayers via the Exchequer, the subsidy is £B'B per unit; in total, rectangle $P_bP_{b'}B'B$ (shaded).

The specific subsidy of £x per unit is B'B; or, on the price axis, $P_b-P_{b'}$. Notice the 'phantom' demand curve D_p. If there had been an autonomous increase in demand and no subsidy, then households would have signalled a demand at B′, forcing the price to rise to P_b, and the quantity supplied to rise to Q_b – the same quantity attributable to the subsidy. The contentious point at issue between the supporters and the opponents of privatization is:

- Should the free market's 'invisible hand' of the price mechanism signal Q_b demand?

OR

- Should civil servants, in part, be the arbiters as they disburse public money which, with the subsidy, also calls forth Q_b demand?

In either case extra resources will be required to shift supply from Q_a to Q_b. These resources will have alternative uses. Can economists offer guidance on how to optimize their use?

The nationalized industries

These are public sector enterprises that produce and sell goods in the market economy.

The NIs had a central role in the economy before privatization: in 1979 they produced more than 10 per cent of the GDP, nearly 20 per cent of capital investment and employed 8 per cent of the labour force. Privatization aims to transfer one million jobs to the private sector and reduce the state industry GDP contribution by half. In 1979 they dominated the energy, communications, steel and transport sectors. To a Labour politician they represent 'the commanding heights of the economy', which the Left would wish to retain in the public sector.

Table 2 itemizes the nationalized industries and public sector firms in rank order of turnover, inherited by the privatizing Conservative administration of 1979. There are additions at the end: the Bank of England which was nationalized in 1946, but is not regarded as an NI; and a clutch of firms, most of which were nationalized by accident rather than by design after they went bankrupt in the market, but were taken over as public assets to keep them trading. Rolls-Royce was a celebrated example, and the Rover Group continues to trade with the help of large government subsidies. The latest casualty, in 1984, was the Johnson Matthey Bank, which the Bank of England purchased for the nominal sum of £1 in order to take control and arrange a rescue package of funds so that the BoE could reassure the nervous money and foreign exchange markets. The BoE privatized JMB in 1986, when it sold it for £40 million.

Table 2   The nationalized industries and public sector firms in 1979

*Nationalized industries,
by rank order of turnover*

  Electricity
  British Telecom
  British Gas
  National Coal Board (Since renamed British Coal)
  British Steel
  British Aerospace
  British Rail
  Post Office
  British Airways
  British Shipbuilders
  National Bus Company
  National Freight Corporation
  British Airports Authority

Renamed corporations
  Britoil (formerly BNOC)
  Enterprise Oil (formerly owned by British Gas)

Miscellaneous firms
  Bank of England
  Rover Group (British Leyland): a quoted company but traded with
    government subsidies
  Rolls-Royce
  Ferranti
  Cable & Wireless
  Amersham International
  Johnson Matthey Bank (added 1984)

Purists would argue, rightly, that the list has been doctored for ease of assimilation. British Telecom and the Post Office were combined in a single corporation until 1980. Britoil and Enterprise Oil did not exist as separate legal entities in 1979; they were renamed for flotation as privatized corporations.

Economic arguments for nationalized industries

Externalities
These can confer social benefits, but they can also impose **social costs**. A market price evaluates only the private cost to the producer and the excludable, rival, private benefit to the purchaser. Its production may, however, be imposing unrecorded social costs on non-consumers.

'Acid rain' – the fallout from emissions of sulphur dioxide from power station chimneys – pollutes the atmosphere, is carried by the prevailing winds and falls on the European continent, visibly affecting buildings and the northern coniferous forests. A nationalized electricity industry could be instructed by the government to install costly filtration equipment to improve the standard of living of our EEC partners. Loss-making rural bus services are kept in existence on government orders. British Rail has loss-making lines which it keeps open because they confer social benefits.

If loss-making is institutionalized then deficit financing requires Exchequer grants to cover the shortfall. When a firm is forced to calculate external costs as well as internal, it 'internalizes' the externality.

Redistribution of income
This is administratively easy if the **public utilities** are nationalized. The essential, basic, household needs of gas, electricity, water and sewerage can be priced below cost to reduce the direct cost of living.

Internalizing externalities is also a way of redistributing income.

Natural monopolies
These are created in a market where, through competition, only one supplier is the outcome. Duplicate pipelines beneath roads for household gas supply would be economically wasteful. The public utilities are natural monopolies: they have **economies of scale**, falling average and marginal costs, with greater capital input and product output. Consumers benefit if prices are correspondingly lower.

In the short run (SR) a saucer-shaped average cost (AC) curve is assumed; some fixed factor causes **diminishing returns** to the variable factor inputs; each successive input of a variable factor produces a diminishing addition to total output. These, when they set in, raise the marginal cost (MC) which, in turn, raises the AC.

In Figure 5 there are five representative **production functions** for a natural monopolist. In the long run, at any given SR stage the factor mix gives SR AC curves which, for the first three from SR_1 to SR_3, give lower costs. In the long run all inputs can be varied so the LR AC falls; the LR **envelope curve** envelopes these SR sequences. Unfortunately, if management coordination and control fail to keep costs down as the scale increases, then in the long run (at SR_4 and SR_5) **diseconomies of scale** set in. This is the 'dinosaur problem' – the body is too big for efficient control, and X-inefficiency from poor internal coordination raises costs from output Q onwards. The LR AC indicates the optimal capacity size, at Q. The SR AC is determined for any given level of capacity.

19

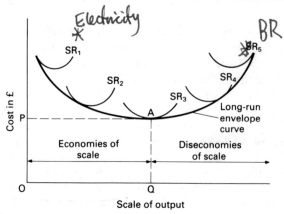

Figure 5 The long-run envelope curve

In Figure 6 the market is supplied, initially, by many firms and their aggregate market supply curve is S_c. This competition produces price P_c where supply and demand are equal at C. If, after mergers and take-overs, a natural monopolist emerges, capable of achieving economies of scale, then the new marginal cost curve (MC_n) produces, even with profit maximization, at W, where $MC_n = MR$, a higher quantity Q_n and a lower price P_n. These are the gains for the consumer.

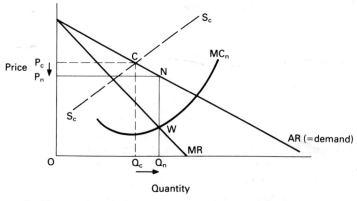

Figure 6 Economies of scale

It is feasible for nationalized industries to offer the gain of economies of scale in theory, but diseconomies in practice. Mismanagement could arise from low-calibre entrepreneurs; but a likely explanation, as we shall soon see, could be government interference overriding the commercial judgement of the industries' managers. This would raise costs above MC_n in Figure 6. The government would be the cause of X-inefficiency.

Profit maximization

A profit-maximizing, private sector, natural monopolist would redistribute income from consumers to shareholders because it would choose a higher price.

It would choose an output where the marginal cost equals the marginal revenue, at point W in Figure 7. The shaded rectangle P_wRFT shows the profit. Note the downward-sloping curves which indicate economies of scale: to reduce the AC the MC must be below it. As there is a sole supplier, the AR curve for the monopolist is society's market demand curve; it is, therefore, downward-sloping. With output Q_w and with MC equal to MR, then the appropriate price is horizontally from R on the demand curve. The AC is cut at point F, so the total cost $OTFQ_w$ is less than revenue.

A nationalized natural monopolist could be instructed to give the monopoly profit to the Exchequer for the betterment of its public sector shareholders – society in general. But is output Q_w optimizing society's resources, and is price P_w the 'right' price?

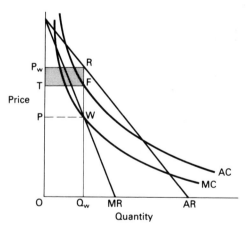

Figure 7 Monopoly profit

OR :

Breaking even

Alternatively the NI could be instructed by the government to 'break even' (i.e. to cover costs but not make any profit). In Figure 8 demand is no longer at R, on the demand curve, but expands to X because of the lower price P_x. X marks the break-even point where revenue (OP_x times OQ_x) equals costs (Q_x times XQ_x). Consumers get a greater output (Q_wQ_x extra) at the lower price (P_wP_x smaller).

However, factor markets will need to supply extra resource inputs for this, for which there will be an **opportunity cost** – the output foregone from the next best alternative use. What is the 'best' use?

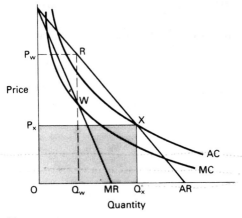

Figure 8 Breaking even

OR

Price equal to marginal cost

A third possibility is to set P equal to MC at Y, in Figure 9, conforming to a cherished ideal of economic theory. Let us see why.

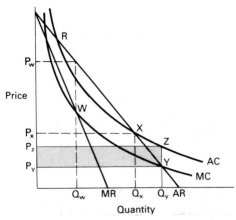

Figure 9 Marginal cost pricing

If the demand curve is a true reflection of society's evaluation of a good – subject to warnings of inequitable income distribution and the market's rigid need for effective, not desired, demand – then the price is equal to the marginal utility (MU) of the last unit consumed. Prices are not on a sliding scale to reflect higher marginal utility for preceding quantities: consumers gain a **consumer surplus** on these.

If the marginal cost curve is a true reflection of society's evaluation of the resource opportunity cost of supply – subject to warnings of distorted evaluation if social costs and benefits are omitted – then the price, *if it is equal to MC*, shows that

$$P = MU = MC.$$

Adam Smith's virtuous 'invisible hand' price mechanism produces a balanced equation of demand equals supply. Hence

$$MU = MC$$

for the last unit demanded and for the last unit supplied.

Moreover, the opportunity cost may be important because society wants an **optimal output** of competing goods and services, requiring scarce factors of production as inputs. Then, in a two-product world (a and b), where

$$\frac{P_a}{P_b} = \frac{MU_a}{MU_b} = \frac{MC_a}{MC_b},$$

an optimal balance exists. To transfer resources from a to b, or from b to a, sub-optimizes society's benefits from its factors of production.

An optimal balance exists when a perfect market long-run outcome has been reached. This is so in Figure 10. Examine the figure and see if you agree with the statements on page 24.

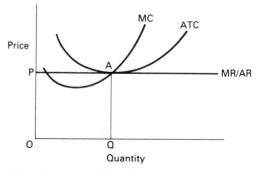

Figure 10 Optimal resource allocation

- Price P is equal to marginal cost at A.
- Price equals marginal utility on the last unit bought, at Q.
- Price equals marginal revenue at A.
- The total costs are OPAQ.
- The total revenue is OPAQ.
- Because total costs.equal total revenue, there can be no supernormal profit.
- If costs include the opportunity cost, then the market is efficient because opportunity cost is covered.
- Any short-run supernormal profit is bid away in the long run as new firms enter. Only normal profit can be made.
- Supernormal profit is a healthy short-run market signal asking for resources to be reallocated into this market.
- There are no barriers to entry or exit, so misallocation does not take place.
- If the above is correct then power lies with the consumer. Consumer sovereignty rules.

Conclusions

See p.36

What does all this imply for the public sector?

- There are no market prices for public goods nor for most public sector merit goods. We are left wondering what is the optimal quantity to supply, the right input of scarce factors of production to use.

- For nationalized industries, it is clear that the monopoly profit with price OP_w in Figure 7 gives a price greater than MC by the magnitude PP_w. The optimization rule is not achieved.

- When P = MC at Y in Figure 9, and optimization is achieved, the falling AC curve of economies of scale leads straight into a very nasty problem. The shaded rectangle of surplus cost is above market revenue OP_yYQ_y. Marginal-cost pricing causes large deficits. It produces loss-making nationalized industries.

The theory has thrown up some tricky problems for the mixed economy and for economists. We want an efficient and equitable allocation and distribution of resources. Do we use markets or government? The post-war consensus held government to be superior for certain goods, these being public goods, merit goods and natural monopolies. However, the same problems still arise: how can we know what consumers want; how can we produce without X-inefficiency; what is an efficient quantity?

KEY WORDS

Public sector	Standard of living
Gross domestic product	Social wage
Relative price effect	Nationalized industries
Transfer payments	Social costs
Public good	Public utilities
Externality	Economies of scale
Impure public good	Diminishing returns
Merit good	Production function
Welfare state	Envelope curve
Mixed economy	Diseconomies of scale
Desired demand	Opportunity cost
Effective demand	Consumer surplus
Lorenz curve	Optimal output

Reading list

Grant and Shaw, 'Role of government in the UK economy' in *Current Issues in Economic Policy*, Philip Allan, 1981.

Griffiths and Wall, 'The nationalized industries' in *Applied Economics*, Longman, 1986.

Harbury, 'Economic welfare' in *Introduction to Economic Behaviour*, Allen & Unwin, 1980.

Hartley, 'Why do governments intervene in the economy?' in *Problems of Economic Policy*, Allen & Unwin, 1977.

Essay topics

1. When should the state be an entrepreneur?
2. 'Any policy which reduces the tax burden and moves the country back towards a *laissez faire* economy must be good.' Argue your case.
3. 'Subsidies distort the price mechanism, so Adam Smith's invisible hand cannot work properly.' Is this true?
4. 'Better that the government should rob the rich than Robin Hood should.' Why?

Data response question 2

Pricing problems in a nationalized industry

The firm represented in the diagram is nationalized and follows a marginal cost pricing policy.

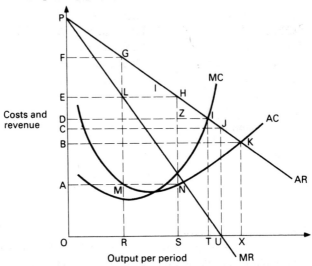

Output per period

(Reproduced with the permission of the University of London School Examinations Board)

1. With specific reference to the diagram, comment on the relationship between price elasticity of demand and marginal revenue.
2. What price would a nationalized industry charge and what output would it produce if pursuing a marginal cost pricing policy?
3. State the change in price that would occur if the firm were to adopt an average-cost pricing policy.
4. (a) What is meant by 'consumer surplus'?
   (b) Assume (i) the firm is now privatized and, instead of following a policy of marginal cost pricing, it follows a policy of profit maximization; and (ii) cost conditions are unchanged and the firm charges the same price to all consumers. What is the change in consumer surplus?
5. Subsequently, if this firm were to pursue a policy of price discrimination, explain with the aid of a diagram how profits could be increased.
6. Examine the circumstances in which a nationalized firm following a marginal cost pricing policy would incur a loss. Use a diagram to illustrate your answer.

Chapter Three

The public sector in practice

'Public expenditure is more like a curate's egg than a shrinking cake' Chancellor of the Exchequer, Nigel Lawson

Preliminaries

Since the establishment of the welfare state and the majority of the nationalized industries in the immediate post-war period, economic problems have changed and so have attitudes. Britain's realization that its economic problems have, in the eyes of the EEC partners, provoked the phrase 'the English disease', has led to a reappraisal of our institutions and economic policies. After offering so many false cures, our economic policy-makers have now turned their attention to a critical evaluation of the public sector.

A basic economic problem for them is that, if the public sector grows bigger as a proportion of the GDP, then private sector consumption, investment and exports are correspondingly lower unless economic growth is sufficiently large to allow the private sector to increase *absolutely* while this *relative* shift takes place.

Figure 11 is a schematic **production possibility curve** at full employment output showing the trade-off between the shares of output for the public versus the private sectors: in media language, for non-economists, shares of the *national cake*. If the proportion of the GDP for the public sector rises, then the shift from A to B reduces the private sector by $X_a - X_b$. Correspondingly the public sector share rises by $Y_b - Y_a$ as resources are shifted into it.

If economic growth is positive then it *is* possible to have the national cake and eat it – in the sense that a shift from A to C gives more public sector output as well as extra $(X_c - X_a)$ private sector output. There is no trade-off, no direct opportunity cost, in the sense that one must fall to allow the other to rise.

Unfortunately, the **recession** of 1980/82 brought a fall in GDP, and output shrank to D. The public sector increased from A to D (i.e. OY_a to OY_b) but the fall in the private sector was dramatic, from X_a to X_d. What the Chancellor and Mrs Thatcher's government wanted was a shrinking *piece* of the national cake for the public sector. What it got

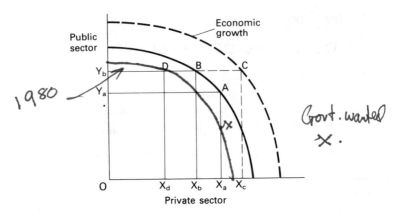

Figure 11 Production possibility curve

was a shrinking national cake with a *bigger* proportion – 47 per cent – for the public sector's expenditure. It achieved the opposite of what it wanted.

All good cakes require eggs. A curate's egg is only good in parts. Why was the Chancellor of the Exchequer so critical of *parts* of public expenditure?

Phantom demand curve
We have already seen in Figure 4 that subsidies alter resource allocation because a 'phantom' demand has been created by government decision rather than by consumer sovereignty. Conservative governments tend to favour the market in preference to Whitehall and town-hall decision-making. In 1984, struggling to close the over-packed suitcase of public expenditure, the government cut back its Regional Policy subsidy support to areas of higher than national average unemployment.

Crowding out
An endorsement of this critical attitude was given academic respectability in the 1960s by the work of two Oxford economists, Bacon and Eltis, who accused the public sector of resource **crowding out**. Expansion of the public sector at that time, especially in health and in education, they argued, pre-empted labour which could be used more effectively in manufacturing industry.

In fact employment in manufacturing has fallen every year since 1966, which makes this thesis look highly questionable. Moreover, public sector services recruited women; manufacturing is traditionally associated with male jobs. No matter, politicians are more comfortable with myths, which support their prejudices.

Sleight of hand: which is correct?

or relatively (%)

A government can cut public expenditure *absolutely*. This is what the Thatcher government wanted to do, but failed to. As the dole queues lengthened so expenditure on unemployment benefit and supplementary benefit rose. To this was then added enormous sums on job subsidies and the Youth Training Scheme. Public expenditure's proportion of the GDP rose to 47 per cent in 1982.

A government can cut public expenditure *relatively* (Figure 13) while it can still be rising absolutely (Figure 12). This looks like sleight of hand

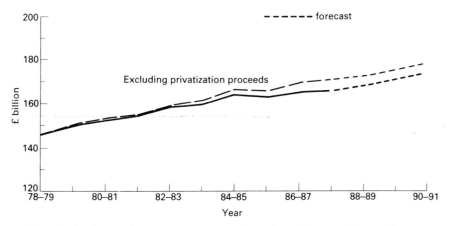

Figure 12   General government expenditure in real terms (*Economic Progress Report* 1987)

– but if the GDP is rising faster than public expenditure then the relative proportion of the GDP taken by public expenditure *will* change: it will fall. This is the strategy the Thatcher government decided to switch to in its Autumn statement of 1986. In terms of sleight of hand, public expenditure can be cut in two ways, absolutely or relatively.

The welfare state

The expansion of health facilities and education in the 1970s produced many jobs and a growing wage bill for the DHSS (health) and local authorities (education). The NHS is Europe's biggest labour user: it employs 100 000 doctors and 450 000 nurses. Before 1979 there were half a million school teachers. With the **demographic change** to fewer

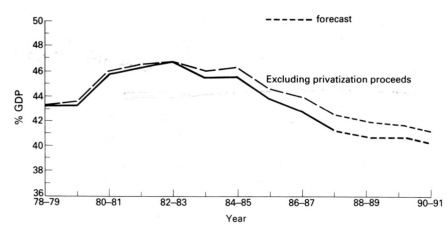

Figure 13 General government expenditure as a percentage of GDP (*Economic Progress Report* 1987)

school-age pupils, the local authorities were subjected to cutbacks in education spending by central government. The authorities reacted by employing fewer teachers, so pupil–teacher ratios have not been maintained: there are now fewer teachers to a given number of pupils. Former teachers of economics may well be joining the growing band of buskers on the London Underground system. Alarming stories have been added by the media of textbook shortages, forcing the sharing of essential texts between groups of pupils.

The health service, too, is the victim of a steady, changing demographic pressure; the population structure indicates ageing in the sense that the absolute numbers of elderly will continue to rise. *Ceteris paribus*, older people consume greater quantities of health care per person. This 'population time bomb' will feature again in Chapter 5.

Although NHS spending has risen in real terms, since 1979, it has not done so by enough to cope with the cost of high-technology medicine and the rising number of the elderly. The administrators in the hospitals have reacted by lengthening the queues for operations. Where the government had hoped for greater efficiency, it has got consumer disbenefit. The College of Health reported 750 000 people waiting for operations in the Spring of 1988; of a total of about 50 000 urgent cases, 30 000 have been waiting longer than one month. More than a quarter of the people on the waiting list have been waiting for more than a year.

The transfer payments of the welfare state – **social security benefits** – we have already calculated as 27 per cent of total government expendi-

An underfunded, more efficient health service? (Reproduced with the kind permission of Richard Willson)

ture. Before proceeding *it is essential to answer a series of simple questions based on Table 3*; this exercise will produce figures and trends, to be used here and in subsequent chapters. The answers will enable you to gauge the number of recipients involved and the large sums of money required.

Pension benefits
(a) Estimate, in round terms, the percentage change from 1979 to 1987. *(b) 11 000 → 22 000 = +100%*
(b) What was the rounded figure for 1987? *22 000*
(c) How many recipients were there in 1987? *22 000*
(d) What has been the trend in recipient numbers since 1979? *Upwardly.*

Unemployment benefit (the 'dole')
(a) The trend in recipients since 1979? *Almost doubled*
(b) The total of recipients in 1987? *935 000*

Supplementary allowances
(a) Number of recipients in 1979?
(b) Number of recipients in 1987?
(c) Rounded figures for cost in 1979?
(d) Rounded figures for cost in 1987?

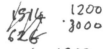

From 1988 the new name for this, which is paid to the unemployed after one year, when unemployment benefit ceases, is *income support*.

Amidst the jungle of benefits in Table 3 you will see Family Income Supplement (to be known, from 1988 onwards, as Family Credit), and Housing Benefit. To protect the lower paid the state provides a safety net of cash to the lower paid, or benefits in kind – Housing Benefit – when rates for house owners or rents for council and private tenants are reduced if families' incomes are below a given threshold. Not shown in the table are costs of free school meals for the children of the lower paid.

Figure 14 shows the net income per week for an average low-paid

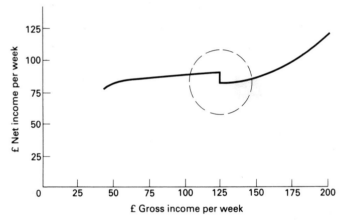

Figure 14 The poverty trap

family: the horizontal axis measures the income *before* tax. If the gross income increases from £110 to £130 the family should be better off, but it clearly is not. Its net income crosses a threshold and it is caught in the **poverty trap**, whereby a £1 gross income increase moves the household to a greater than 100 per cent marginal tax rate. The paradox needs an explanation.

The nominal cash gain of £20 is offset by the loss of benefits in kind. The household is required now to pay for school meals; FIS is withdrawn and they pay a higher rent – so the new outgoings are greater than the new income.

The public sector in practice

Table 3 Social security benefits: public expenditure and estimated numbers of recipients (*Social Trends* 1987)

	Expenditure (£ million)				Recipients (thousands)			
	79–80	84–85	85–86	86–87	79–80	84–85	85–86	86–87
NATIONAL INSURANCE BENEFITS								
Pension benefits								
Retirement pensions	8 816	15 307	16 677	17 776	8 680	9 350	9 445	9 525
Invalidity benefit	995	2 153	2 373	2 617	620	825	870	910
Industrial disablement benefit	244	381	396	408	200	185	180	175
Widow's benefits and industrial death benefit	599	836	869	902	520	455	445	435
Lump-sum payment to contributory pensioners	96	105	105	106	9 600	10 400	10 500	10 600
Other benefits								
Unemployment benefit	653	1 578	1 597	1 618	550	1 020	965	935
Sickness benefits	655	279	296	123	490	180	180	60
Death grant	16	17	17	18	600	610	620	600
Maternity allowance	125	161	173	183	115	120	115	125

NON-CONTRIBUTORY BENEFITS

Pension benefits

Non-contributory retirement pensions	36	39	39	38	55	35	35	30
War pensions	375	544	560	572	370	305	295	285
Attendance allowance and invalid care allowance	205	587	681	766	290	500	555	595
Severe disablement allowance	85	232	228	260	165	225	230	245
Mobility allowance	79	356	430	507	140	355	400	450
Lump-sum payments to non-contributory pensioners	5	6	6	7	500	600	600	700
Other benefits								
Supplementary pensions	895	873	1 008	997	1 720	1 735	1 765	1 805
Supplementary allowances	1 541	5 578	6 200	6 267	1 200	2 930	3 030	3 030
Child benefit	2 787	4 276	4 397	4 425	13 330	12 430	12 210	12 035
Family income supplement	27	126	136	158	80	205	205	215
One-parent benefit	43	120	134	148	370	565	590	615
Maternity grant	16	18	17	18	660	740	700	700
Housing benefit – rent rebates and allowances	278	2 823	3 068	3 154	1 425	4 910	5 020	5 010
ADMINISTRATIVE AND MISCELLANEOUS SERVICES	837	1 743	1 807	1 858				

(Reproduced with the permission of the Controller of HMSO)

For some families the net increase in income before £100 is so small that voluntary unemployment and an income from social security benefits might be preferable to poorly paid work. This is the **unemployment trap**, all too clearly seen in the extract from the *Daily Mail* shown in Figure 15.

A free hotel for handout family

AN Irishman who has never worked is living with his family on £160 a week social security in a hotel paid for by a council.

James Joyce, his wife Margaret, and their four children were put up at the Kensington International, West London – where bed and breakfast is about £55 a night – by Brent Council.

Yesterday, when Mrs Joyce appeared barefooted at Horseferry Road Court on a drunkenness charge, magistrate Mr Eric Crowther asked her who was paying for the hotel.

When she told him Brent, he said: 'Oh yes – you are a bit unlucky not to get into the Hilton.'

Admitted

The 27-year-old Belfast-born housewife admitted being drunk in charge of her 12-month-old son, James. Her cousin, 26-year-old Dubliner Mary Joyce – who is also staying in a hotel – admitted being drunk in charge of her five-year-old son, Patrick.

Both women were seen outside an Earls Court pub at 8.45 pm with James in a pushchair and other children nearby playing with rubbish.

Later, after the two were bailed for reports, Margaret said Brent put her and her family into a Paddington hotel when they arrived homeless from Belfast five months ago. Five weeks ago, they transferred to the Kensington International so the children could be near a school.

'It's lovely in the hotel,' she added. 'We're really enjoying it.'

Figure 15 The unemployment trap
(Reproduced with the permission of Mail Newspapers plc)

Public expenditure is more like a curate's egg if it creates poverty and unemployment traps. It is publicly-created disbenefits like these, and what they perceive as the inefficiencies of the nationalized industries, that have prejudiced the Thatcher government against public provision and created their desire to roll back the frontier of the public sector.

The nationalized industries

Despite the pricing problems encountered in the public sector, in theory the NIs should be exempt from these because they have a mechanism for evaluating and meeting consumer demand – the price mechanism. Although the original statutes which created them were rather vague on what their goals should be, two White Papers in the 1960s put them on course. The latest, in 1978, was quite specific on two important points, which we shall now examine.

The White Paper pricing policy

In Figures 7, 8 and 9, there was a pricing dilemma left unresolved. The White Paper gave the solution – a fourth alternative, **long-run marginal cost pricing**.

Turn back to Figure 5, the envelope curve. Find price P and output Q; associated with these is point A where, in the long run, prices are at their lowest, P. Then P = long run MC at A. Any intermediate output and price associated with SR$_1$ or SR$_2$ would not conform to the 1978 rule. It would represent a short-run journey on the way to the long-run marginal cost goal, given that demand will reach this point. Expanding electricity can try to achieve this aim; contracting British Rail would be expected to reduce capital by disinvestment, and so reduce costs to get down to long-run marginal cost policy from SR$_4$ or SR$_5$.

Two pricing problems

The first problem is that the public utilities do not face a standard demand curve – they have a *peak load* problem. Within a 24-hour cycle there are wild swings in demand. What would you consider the marginal cost to be of one extra passenger on a commuter train that is half empty at, say, 1400 hours?

Price discrimination is used for telephones, rail and electricity. Different prices at different times help to spread the load. Flexible buyers choose the cheaper 'off-peak' prices, so their demand is *price elastic*.

The second problem is that powerful vested interest groups of local MPs, trade unions and, sometimes, the NIs themselves expect the NIs to allow for social benefits, such as keeping open 'uneconomic' railway lines, shipyards where the local unemployment rate is very high and – until the miners lost their year-long dispute of 1984 – 'uneconomic' pits. The 1968 White Paper rejected **cross-price subsidies** – which, using higher prices on profitable sectors of a business, could be used to raise enough revenue to carry loss-making sectors – in favour of specific subsidies from the Treasury. Figure 4 makes an analysis of this principle.

The White Paper investment policy

The 1978 White Paper brought in a new *required rate of return* on existing capital assets, because investment appraisal methods had been

over-optimistic in the expectations that had been calculated to justify
producing these assets.

 Better productive efficiency was the aim, coupled with the pricing
policy that we have looked at. Short-run marginal cost pricing equates
immediate marginal costs and marginal benefits. In the long run, if
efficient investment decisions are made, then capacity is adjusted to
ensure that this price also reflects the long-run marginal opportunity
cost of that capital.

 The Treasury has issued comparative details for private industry and
the nationalized industries of real rates of return. A glance at Figure 16
gives ammunition to the privatizers.

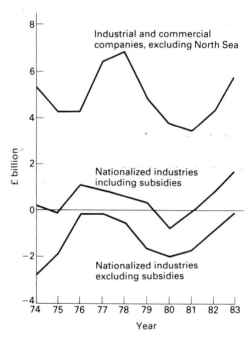

Figure 16 Real rates of return for the main nationalized industries
(*Economic Progress Report*, June/July 1985)

Tarnished silver?

Enthusiasts for privatization claim that the rate of return on existing
and on new capital for former NIs will rise as a consequence of transfer
of ownership. If privatized firms are unable to finance negative- or
low-return investment projects then this claim is self-evidently correct.

 Critics gloomily predict an even lower figure for the remaining rump of NIs because only the better achievers are being sold off – a case of sell the best silver and keep the tarnished, perhaps?

NEDO's study of UK nationalized industries

A National Economic Development Office report published in 1976 studied nine major nationalized corporations (omitting aerospace, shipbuilding and airports) from the list in Table 2 on page 18. The report may be summarized in three sections.

Central role in the economy
To quote the report: 'The way the NIs use the resources they control is a matter of prime national concern.'

Problems of control
The Acts of Parliament which established each industry expected an 'arms length' approach by ministers. The industries were to be left to the managers for day-to-day running, with official White Papers to lay down guidelines. In the 1970s both major political parties when in government were **interventionist**: the day-to-day priorities of the industries were overridden by ministerial orders designed to achieve political gain rather than economic advantage. The most notorious was the price restraint imposed on them which merely created **suppressed inflation**, an exercise in economic delusion by Whitehall.

'Whitehall' is the standard metaphor for government departments, many of which are in buildings along this street, near Parliament. The 'dead hand of Whitehall' features in a later data response question (at the end of Chapter 4). Critics regard 'the invisible hand' of competition as preferable.

The NEDO report admitted: 'Policies of price restraint made the targets and requirement to base price on long-run marginal costs largely irrelevant.' Such was the muddle, dislocation and turmoil that NEDO observed, sadly, that the relationship between governments and the NIs had deteriorated into 'mutual recrimination' and the outcome was 'a minimizing environment' with few rewards for real success'.

The 'mutual recrimination' can still surface. A *Sunday Telegraph* article revealed that the Chairman of British Coal, who lunched at 10 Downing Street, was exposed to 'relentless criticism' from the lady incumbent: 'We probably went along on the wrong day . . . I have weals on my back.'

Would this interference be tolerated as the way to run ICI or Marks and Spencer?

The Treasury ministers can be the worst monopolists of all. During periods of tight public expenditure control they instructed the nationalized industries to raise prices. This meant the loss-makers reduced their dependence on subsidies and the profit-makers increased their monopoly profits – which were then paid to the Treasury.

The NEDO report: its importance and relevance to privatization
The report publicized convincingly the problems of the NIs:

'The evidence points overwhelmingly to the conclusion that relationships between governments and nationalized industries can have damaging economic consequences for the country as a whole.'

NEDO prepared the ground for change:

'. . . the relationship between government and the nationalized industries is a matter of major significance; its effect for good or ill on the country's industrial performance can hardly be exaggerated. Our enquiry has left us in no doubt that the existing framework of relationships is unsatisfactory and in need of radical change.

Within three years of this being written a government was elected, in 1979, which believed that the public sector was good only in parts – like the curate's egg – and that the other parts were in need of radical change. This change was to be brought about by a forceful programme of privatization.

KEY WORDS

Production possibility curve	Long-run marginal cost
Recession	Price discrimination
Crowding out	Cross price subsidies
Demographic change	NEDO
Social security benefits	Interventionist
Poverty trap	Suppressed inflation
Unemployment trap	

Reading list

The Economist, 'Supervising state industries' in *Britain's Business*, Economist Newspapers Ltd, 1986, pp. 4–5.
Harbury and Lipsey, 'Government and resource allocation' in *An Introduction to the UK Economy*, Pitman, 1986.

Hare and Kirby, 'Nationalized industries' in *British Economic Policy*, Wheatsheaf, 1984.

Hartley, 'Monopoly, bureaucracy and competition in the public sector' in *Problems of Economic Policy*, Allen & Unwin, 1977.

Prest and Coppock, 'The nationalized industries' in *The UK Economy*, Weidenfeld, 1986.

Smith, 'Reining back the public sector' in *Mrs Thatcher's economics*, Heinemann Educational Books, 1988.

Essay topics

1. Should the nationalized industries behave like private sector industries?
2. 'A natural monopoly is a natural part of the public sector.' True?
3. 'Public expenditure is more like a curate's egg than a shrinking cake.' What does this mean and is it true?

Data response question 3

Treasury new boy must hit target

Understandably, many readers skip this kind of newspaper article (taken from *The Times* of 2 September 1985). For an A-level student it makes interesting reading in applied economics. All the questions below are based on what has been covered in this chapter.

1. 'Standing in the way of this target are the spending departments.' Give a functional list.
2. 'Excess bids of about £4 billion.' If the government succeeds in eliminating this excess, what is the trade-off for the consumer? Is it good or bad?
3. What four categories are the reason for the overshoot?
4. Classify these into economic categories.
5. What is 'the second reason for the Treasury's optimism?'

Why Treasury new boy must hit £139bn target

September, with its first hints of autumn, marks the end of the phoney war on public spending. The officials have done their work while ministers were away enjoying themselves in Cannes or Conservative Party summer school. Now, battle will commence.

The public spending round will start slowly, with low-key bilateral meetings, building up to a crescendo late in October with tales of blood on the Chief Secretary's carpet, fraught sessions in the Star Chamber and bitter rows in Cabinet. Somehow, it always ends in tears.

This year, apart from the prospect of a more difficult round than usual, added interest will be generated by Mrs Thatcher's Cabinet reshuffle, and the likelihood of a new man in the post of Chief Secretary to the Treasury.

Mr Peter Rees, the present incumbent, has, it must be admitted, been tipped for the sack more times than Tommy Docherty. This time it does appear that he will have to hang up his public spending axe.

What task does the new Chief Secretary, barring a Houdini-like escape by Mr Rees, face? The goal is the achievement of an overall public spending planning total of £139 billion for next year, 1986/87. This target was reaffirmed at the July Cabinet meeting on public spending.

Standing in the way of this target are the spending departments, who would like rather more. Treasury officials who do not calculate in such a vulgar way would, if pressed, say that the level of excess bids currently adds up to about £4 billion. This is slightly more than the £3.5 billion fiscal adjustment, or tax cut, that the Treasury has pencilled in for the next Budget.

There are four main items in the present total for excess bids. Higher inflation than the Treasury had predicted has had the effect of boosting the cost of programmes next year by about £1 billion. The bulk of this arises out of the 7 per cent uprating of pensions and related rises in other social security benefits from November, partly offset by a real cut in the value of child benefit and some savings associated with the Fowler social security review.

The second important item is local authority spending, on which the Treasury has conceded an extra £500 million. This amount, on current spending, is a relatively small concession compared with previous years. However, the Treasury believes that the Department of the Environment's new system for controlling town hall spending should prevent a further request for local authority cash at this stage.

Another £500 million arises out of higher unemployment than was assumed in the public spending plans, together with increased take-up of social security benefits. The public spending White Paper, published in January, assumed adult unemployment constant at three million until 1987/88.

The unemployment figures published on Friday showed adult unemployment in August at 3,182,200, well above the assumed total. For every 100,000 that unemployment is above three million, public spending can be expected to rise by £200 million a year.

The fourth big item is the state industries. Coal, in particular, is taking a long time to recover from the financial damage inflicted by the miners' strike, while there have also been permanent effects on rail traffic. The result is that state industries taken as a whole are unlikely to come near the relatively optimistic targets that the Treasury has set them.

41

The total external finance of the state industries is targeted to drop to just £178 million in 1986/87, from a January target of £1.3 billion for this year and well over £3 billion last. Next year's target now looks even more unrealistic and will have to be raised by up to £1 billion.

These four items – inflation, local authorities, unemployment and state industries – add up to almost £3 billion of the £4 billion of excess bids. And here lies the difficulty with this year's round, this £3 billion is a 'hard' figure, as much as these things can ever be.

When other uncertainties such as the size of the eventual teachers' pay settlement are taken on board, it is surprising to discover that the Treasury is privately quite confident of holding the public spending line, admittedly after a difficult round, and sticking with the £139 billion target.

Part of the reason for this confidence on the part of the Treasury is the Chancellor's decision, taken at Budget-time at the end of the year-long coal strike, to add £2 billion to the reserve for 1985/86 and the two subsequent years.

Because of this, the Treasury has a substantial cushion, in the form of a £6 billion reserve for 1986/87, in this year's public spending discussions.

The second reason is that next year's asset sales are likely to be much bigger in total than in existing plans. The published target is for the so-called special sales of assets to raise just £2.2 billion in 1986/87.

That target was set before the launching of the programme to privatize British Gas, which could raise £2 billion on its own next year, as the first of what will probably be four such payments. The third and final payment on British Telecom shares will bring in another £1.2 billion, and now it looks as if British Airways too will be sold off next year.

A further increase in the current round would not only remove some of the scope for tax reductions, but cost dearly in terms of credibility, as well.

David Smith
Economics Correspondent

Chapter Four

Privatization in theory

'Privatization is seen as a way of reasserting consumer sovereignty, raising standards of provision, of increasing efficiency and of reducing costs.' J. R. Shackleton

---

Denationalization, deregulation and franchising are all methods of privatization (see Figure 1), although D. R. Pendse claims that: 'Any process that reduces involvement of the state or the public sector in a nation's activities, is, in my view, a privatization'.

The benefits of privatization

None of the standard arguments for nationalization which I outlined on pages 18–24 can be regarded as incontrovertible.

- *Natural monopolies* can be in the private sector, as they are in the USA. Consumer interests are protected by a regulatory body.

- *Externalities* can be dealt with through recourse to the law, the use of subsidies or the imposition of taxes.

- *Income redistribution* is achieved more efficiently through direct income transfer, using transfer payments. Under-pricing nationalized industry outputs is a crude mechanism which is unselective in its impact. It also misallocates resources. There is no obvious size for the public sector. Many of the nationalized industries are the outcome of political zeal, rather than dispassionate economics. With a higher standard of living much the same can now be argued about the welfare state – a Universal Provider State is by no means necessary in the affluent late twentieth century.

Privatization benefits are considered to be fourfold, two major and two minor. We shall look at the major ones first.

① Political interference prevents the achievement of target rates of return. We have already studied the onslaught on 'the damaging economic consequences for the country' mounted by NEDO, in its study of UK nationalized industries (page 39). A privatized sector is a more *independent* sector.

② State monopolies create inefficiency, are poor in innovation and

43

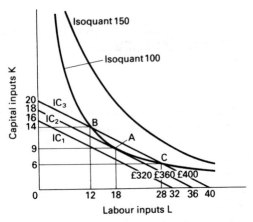

Figure 17 Productive efficiency of a firm

restrict consumer choice; instead of the consumer being sovereign, power has been transferred to the state and its bureaucracies. Privatization has the potential – depending upon the form it takes – for *widening consumer choice*, giving a better quality of service, lower prices and for the whole of society a better, *more efficient use of its resources*.

For economists there are two aspects to efficiency. **Allocative efficiency** occurs when price equals marginal cost. This was considered on page 22. In such circumstances the sovereign with the power is the consumer. Resources are allocated in accordance with changes in consumer preferences and society's resources are at optimal use. For product prices to reflect the cost of provision, barriers to entry and exit of firms should not exist.

Productive efficiency occurs when a firm minimizes the cost of a given level of output. A profit maximizer automatically seeks productive efficiency, (even in Figure 7 on page 21). This concept is best illustrated with isoquants and isocosts, as in Figure 17.

An **isoquant** is an equal-output curve. It indicates the combinations of two factor inputs, say capital (K) and labour (L), which can, with given technology, produce a stated output. It is non-linear because one factor is not a perfect substitute for the other. The marginal rate of substitution changes one for the other – if the aim is to maintain a stated output then the slope of the isoquant changes with their ratios.

An **isocost** line is a firm's budget line. Its shape is derived from the relative prices of the factors of production. In Figure 17, capital is priced at £20 per unit and labour at £10 per unit, so isocost IC_1 is plotted at 16 (= £320) on the y-axis and 32 (= £320) on the x-axis. If the aim is to produce output 100, then IC_1 at £320 spends too little to reach it. At B the capital required is 14 (= £280) and labour 12 (= £120), so the cost of 100 outputs is £400. Check 6K and 28L at C to confirm that this is so. A is productively efficient because the price, with 9K and 18L, is reduced to £360.

There are two further, minor, privatization benefits. Firstly there is *wider shareholding*. The well-publicized sale of familiar state assets, at prices which are attractive to Everyman, can reverse a trend that has been causing concern. The small percentage of the populace owning shares directly had become so small that commentators had regarded this trend as a weakness of capitalism. At its most simplistic a wider share-owning democracy could be a pro-capitalist democracy. This is, incidentally, hardly an argument for privatization, as such, more a circular argument for wider share-owning.

The second minor benefit concerns the *public sector borrowing requirement* (**PSBR**). This is the sum which, each year, central government has to fund for itself, the local authorities and the nationalized industries when they need to borrow because expenditure is greater than income. After privatization, any financial capital required by a former state sector enterprise – for new capital investment in factory capacity or plant and machinery – will have to be raised on the private market and will no longer be supplied by the Treasury. Moreover, if each year there are profit taxes from the privatized firms then that years' PSBR can be lower too.

Criteria for privatization

Lest it now be thought that

> Privatization is Good
> and
> State provision is Bad

pause for a moment and reflect on the concept of public goods – which the state provides and produces because the market would under-produce.

For goods and services which are both rival and excludable (refer back to page 11), let us introduce the word **pragmatism**. This approach is used in the UK by the Monopolies and Mergers Commission. It scrutinizes a case on its merits; there are no hard and fast rules.

The criteria to justify privatization are such that pragmatism becomes the deciding factor: look at each case on its merits and seek out the **aggregate net benefits** to the consumer, both directly and indirectly. Beesley and Littlechild (consult the reading list) mention the following:

45

- lower prices
- greater output
- better quality and variety
- greater innovation
- changes in the distribution of benefits
- effects on employees, suppliers, exports and taxpayers.

Lest students believe that economic principles can deliver an unequivo-cal 'right' answer, it needs to be stressed that a value judgement is necessary. The approach here singles out the consumer for special favour. I would imagine that, as a consumer, the reader approves of this. At this stage you might turn back to refresh your memory of Mr Edmonds' trade union view that the consumer is the loser, on page 7.

The consumer gains can be summarized as improved allocative efficiency. Privatized entrepreneurs would be motivated to strive for productive efficiency. 'Competition', according to Beesley and Littlechild, 'is the most important mechanism for maximizing consumer benefits.' It follows, therefore, that statutory barriers to entry, put there by Acts of Parliament, should be removed.

It may be thought necessary to impose on some privatized industries non-commercial obligations – a rural post office, rural telephone kiosks, retention of some railway lines that cannot be expected to pay to cover their private costs of production but which confer social benefits to 'justify' their retention. The private benefits measured by the price mechanism under-record their value. Rather than expect **cross-subsidization** whereby one group of consumers pays higher prices to subsidize socially sanctioned outputs, explicit specific subsidies from the taxpayer could be negotiated prior to privatization.

In Figure 18, MPB and MSB are marginal private and social benefit respectively. An equilibrium, without a subsidy, would be a marginal

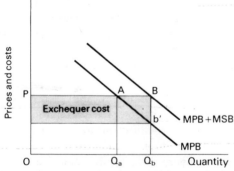

Figure 18 Specific subsidy for privatized output

cost equality at point A, which gives quantity Q_a output. If the taxpayer offers specific subsidy b'B, then the output can rise to Q_b, at an unchanged price of P. The equilibrium is derived at B, where the combined private and social benefits are measured. For comparison see Figure 4, which did not measure social benefit.

Using these criteria, Beesley and Littlechild have examined the major nationalized industries irrespective of whether their demand prospects are good or bad. They conclude that five would give the bulk of the aggregate net benefits, if privatized:

Coal   Electricity   Post   Rail   Telephones

You will probably know already how many of these have *not* been privatized.... 4

Privatization and contestable markets

'The theory of **contestable markets** has now reached a stage when its exciting and already well-established conclusions demand widespread public attention' (Davies and Davies: consult the reading list). Contestability has, like privatization, left the average textbook behind; yet, for some of the natural monopolies, privatization and contestability seem inseparable.

A perfectly contestable market has no **barriers to entry** nor to **exit**: a perfectly competitive market is a contestable market. Not all contestable markets are perfectly competitive markets, however: both oligopolistic and, indeed, pure monopoly markets could be contestable. The number of firms is irrelevant; the key is the force of potential competition, which, even with profit-maximizing firms, will produce an outcome of only **normal profit.**

The deregulation of the London Stock Exchange in 1986 – known as the Big Bang – has increased contestability in the financial markets. Although it was limited to the removal of barriers to entry, the financial conglomerates involved – particularly the banks – because they are so diversified, knew that they could pull out if unsuccessful. This the Midland Bank did, in 1987, when it had lost £25 million dealing as a market-maker in equities. A few weeks later Lloyds Bank left the new gilt-edged securities market.

In the context of privatization, a contestable market could be a natural monopoly with its benefit of economies of scale but without the disbenefit of private sector monopoly profit.

The theory of contestability is summarized in Table 4. You will be familiar with the characteristics of both perfect competition and monopoly. Check these against a contestable market.

Table 4 Basic characteristics of perfectly competitive, perfectly contestable and monopoly markets (Button, 'New approaches to the regulation of industry', *Royal Bank of Scotland Review*, December 1985)

	Competitive	Contestable	Monopoly
Number of firms	Large	Irrelevant	One
Size of firms	Small	Irrelevant	Substantial
Barriers to entry/ exit	None	None	Extensive
Product of firms	Homogeneous	May be diversified	Homogeneous
Profit levels	Normal profits	Normal profits	Monopoly rents
Managerial motivations	Profit maximization	Profit maximization	Normally profit maximization

A natural monopoly may require a huge network of fixed capital, either nationally or regionally. This is so for gas, electricity, the postal service's letter-boxes, offices and vans, the telephone lines and exchanges for telecommunications, British Rail's stations, railway track network and rolling stock. These are the nation's **infrastructure**.

This capital represents a huge **sunk cost**: it is capital without an alternative use which is financially not recoverable. Your sunk cost if you go to the cinema and leave half way through a disappointing film is the cost of the full price of the ticket – you cannot get half its price back for seeing only half the film. The private monopolist firm that has huge sunk costs is locked into an industry, so it has a barrier to exit if the monopolist cannot run it profitably. Simultaneously this barrier to exit is a barrier to entry to a potential entrant: too costly to get in, too costly to get out.

If, when privatizing, the government retained this sunk-cost capital network in public ownership, then it could offer a time-limit franchise to a monopolist entrant based on competitive tender. Failure to make a normal profit after say, five years, would be an inducement for it to leave the industry and be replaced by a new, enfranchised entrant. In this contestable market the successful incumbent monopolist would still only make a normal profit – to make excess profit would attract rivals at franchise renewal.

FRANCHISING NI'S INFRASTRUCTUR
ELIMINATES BARRIERS TO ENTRY

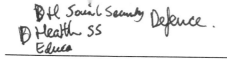

Privatization and the welfare state

You were asked in Chapter 2 to memorize the top four spenders. You may need to refresh your memory from Figure 2.

Omitting defence, combining expenditure by the Department of Health and Social Security with that for education rounds up to what 60% simple percentage? This is the foundation of the welfare state – social security incomes for the sick, unemployed and retired, free health care and education.

Using the economic classifications developed in Chapter 2, these are transfer payment income subsidies, price subsidies (e.g. medical prescriptions) and merit goods to satisfy merit wants. In Figure 14 we studied how the poverty trap catches private sector house tenants who lose their rent rebate (price subsidy) at the threshold indicated.

Market failure is the basis of public provision and public production where needed, of welfare state goods and services. Neither efficiency in production nor fairness in distribution would be the outcome of a *laissez faire* private market. A welfare state produces positive externality gains of a healthier, more productive, literate, more caring, better educated citizenry. Equal treatment in health and education is more equitable.

Contemporary critics argue that a welfare state produces monopolies – the NHS and local catchment-area schools – that merely produce one market failure for another. Large bureaucracies are needed to run these and they are productively inefficient. There is not consumer sovereignty but producer sovereignty.

Privatization proposals include selling off council houses, replacing student grants with loans, and the introduction of **voucher schemes** for school education. Families would 'buy' education at schools of their choice, whether state-run or private, their entitlement to vouchers being a function of income. The government would redeem the vouchers for cash. This would be public provision with either public or private production. Student loans would be private provision with public production.

Figure 19 shows you what privatization could do to your school. Would you support the idea?

Right-wingers in move to sell off state schools

A CONFIDENTIAL Tory party document recommending that state schools should be sold off to private companies is circulating among senior party advisers.

The document, which has appalled Tory 'wets' on the party's education committee, is thought to be the brainchild of the radical Right.

This wing of the party showed last week that it had secured considerable support for privatising education from Downing Street when Mrs Thatcher let it be known that she is considering the introduction of vouchers, bringing back direct grant schools and seeking City money for inner-city schools.

The latest, more sweeping proposals for privatising the education service, suggest that companies should be asked to tender for a package of schools, some urban and some rural, and their results after five years would be compared with those which remained under local authority control. Teachers in company schools would be paid by the company.

The plan has been submitted to the Conservative Central Office, local government and education advisory committees with a request that it should be examined carefully in order that a joint assessment can be made.

The education committee, which has a considerable number of 'wets' among its 100 members, turned down the paper at its quarterly meeting at Central Office. The committee's chairman, Maurice Venn, said last week: 'That is a confidential party document. I cannot comment on it until it stops being confidential.'

But one committee member said he was seriously worried by the paper. 'On one level I think this plan is just ridiculous, but there is a concerted attack at present on the concept of the maintained sector which has the Prime Minister's personal support and which I take very seriously.

'What annoys me is that time and effort is going into producing loony schemes like this when we desperately need to sort out the problems of the maintained sector.'

The paper concedes that the best teachers might be drawn out of state schools into company schools by higher pay. It adds that 'any high pay offered by companies would be tempered by their competitive tendering and the profit motive.' Councils left with bad teachers would simply have to let more schools.

Judith Judd
Education Correspondent
The Observer, 2 March 1986

Figure 19 Privatization in the classroom

We must turn to privatization policy in practice. However, first consider two questions:

● *Can you privatize a loo?* This is not the frivolous question it appears. Consider the loo on platform 8 at British Rail's King's Cross station.

BR has licensed out the site to a private firm. This firm demolished the existing toilet and built an impressive new one. There is a standard charge for entry for all-comers – evidently the answer to the question is in the affirmative – to the gain of the public. It fits the quotation at the heading of this chapter: 'raising standards of provision'.

The moral of this frivolous story is serious economics. It is *not* necessary to 'sell the family silver' when franchising can produce the desired result.

BR is now putting out to tender the franchise for running its Travellers Fare buffets. A BR spokesman denied that this is privatization: he seemed unaware of the wider definition of the word.

• *Can you privatize a prison?* Certainly! In the USA the Corrections Corporation of America has been running profit-making prisons for some years. The externality gains of law and order require this public good to be publicly funded but private production is perfectly possible. Tory MPs are generally enthusiastic. Labour MPs tend to claim that 'prisons for profit' are immoral. What do you think?

KEY WORDS

Allocative efficiency	Contestable market
Productive efficiency	Barriers to entry
Isoquant	Barriers to exit
Isocost	Normal profit
PSBR	Infrastructure
Pragmatism	Sunk cost
Aggregate net benefits	Voucher schemes
Cross-subsidization	

Reading list

Anderton, 'Markets and efficiency' in *Economics: A New Approach*, University Tutorial Press, 1984.

Barker, 'Competition from new entrants' in *Case Studies in the Competitive Process*, Heinemann Educational Books, 1976.

Beesley and Littlechild, 'Privatization: principles, problems and regulation' in Kay, Mayer and Thompson, *Privatization and Regulation*, Oxford University Press, 1986.

Blaug, 'The pros and cons of education vouchers', *Economic Review*, vol. 4, May 1987.

Burningham, 'Markets and efficiency' in *Teach Yourself Economics*, Hodder, 1984.

Charles, 'Arguments for and against council house sales'; 'Voucher systems in education'; 'Medical care and insurance'; in *Case Studies in the Economics of Social Issues*, Heinemann Educational Books, 1979.

Davies and Davies, 'The revolution in monopoly theory', *Lloyds Bank Review*, July 1984, p. 38.

Donaldson, 'Welfare state or going private?' in *A Question of Economics*, Penguin, 1986.

Davis, 'What can we do with the social security system?', *Economic Review*, vol. 3, Sept. 1985.

McDonald, 'Contestable markets – a new ideal model?', *Economics* (The Economics Association), Spring 1987.

Pendse, 'Some Reflections on the Privatization Process' in *National Westminster Quarterly Review*, November 1985.

Robinson, 'Privatization and the welfare state', *Economic Review*, vol. 1, Sept. 1983.

Shackleton, 'Privatization, the Case Examined' in *National Westminster Quarterly Review*, May 1984.

Essay topics

1. 'Privatization is seen as a way of reasserting consumer sovereignty, of raising standards of provision, of increasing efficiency and of reducing costs.' How?
2. 'If British Rail is getting there it would get there even quicker in contestable regional markets.' Consider this claim.
3. 'A private utility is worse than a public utility.' Correct?
4. 'Hands Off the Welfare State! Don't Hang Beveridge. Hang the Privatizers!' What would you do?

Data response question 4

Private utilities

Answer the following questions based on the accompanying tables:

Define PSBR (Table 2)
1. What are (i) public asset sales
              (ii) housing budget capital receipts?
2. What is the significance of the term 'Underlying' PSBR in Table 2?
3. Which items of public expenditure have grown fastest in real terms since 1979/80 (Table 1)? Account for the Government's failure to reduce the level of public expenditure.
4. Why has the PSBR fallen as a proportion of GDP since 1979/80?

5. What are the implications of Table 3 for the Government's economic strategy?

(Reproduced with the permission of the Oxford and Cambridge Schools Examination Board)

Table 1   Major categories of tax receipts at 1985/86 prices[A]

£ million	1979/80	1986/87 (estimate)	% Change
Inland revenue receipts	45 569	55 296	21.3
Customs and excise receipts	29 485	40 039	35.8
National insurance	24 254	25 753	6.2
Local authority rates	11 168	15 053	34.9

Expenditure by department at 1985/86 prices[A]

£ million	1979/80	1986/87 (estimate)	% Change
Planned expenditure on programmes of which:	125 961	140 331	11.4
Defence	14 908	17 687	18.6
Education and science	14 451	15 258	5.6
DHSS – health and personal social services	14 383	17 493	21.6
DHSS – social security	31 367	43 343	38.2

([A]: Adjusted using the GDP deflator)

Table 2   Public sector borrowing

£ million	1979/80	1986/87	1987/88 (Treasury forecast)
PSBR	10 020	3 333	3 900
Public asset sales	337	4 400	5 000
Housing budget capital receipts	472	1 886	1 702
'Underlying' PSBR	10 829	9 619	10 602
PSBR as % of GDP	4.8	0.9	0.9
'Underlying' PSBR as % of GDP	5.2	2.5	2.6

Table 3   General government receipts and expenditure

£ billion	1986/87		1987/88	
	1986 Budget forecast	1987 Budget estimate	1987 Budget forecast	% change
Total taxes and royalties	117.9	119.4	127.8	7.0
of which:				
Income tax	38.7	38.4	40.0	4.2
Corporation tax excluding North Sea	9.4	11.2	13.5	20.5
Value Added Tax	20.7	21.5	23.3	8.4
Local authority rates	15.6	15.5	16.9	9.0
Other expenditure taxes	26.0	26.5	27.6	4.2
North Sea revenues	6.1	4.8	3.9	−18.8
National insurance etc	26.2	26.5	28.5	7.5
Other	11.5	11.7	11.8	0.9
General government receipts	155.6	157.6	168.1	6.7
General government expenditure	164.3	168.9	175.0	3.6

(Source: *Barclays Bank Review*, May 1987)

Chapter Five

Privatization in practice

'We must roll back the frontier of the public sector.' Mrs Margaret
Thatcher

The state of the state's silverware

Using privatization to roll back the frontier of the public sector has been
one of the most vigorously pursued of the Thatcher governments'
policies. Its ambitious scale and gathering momentum may be gauged
from Table 1 in Chapter 1 and from the Treasury's published receipts
(in £ billion) since 1979 (a total of £16 690 million):

1979	1980	1981	1982	1983	1984	1985	1986	1987
0.37	0.40	0.49	0.48	1.10	2.1	2.7	4.4	4.65

The policy affects you directly if you telephone, fly by British Airways,
keep warm with gas central heating, travel by motorway bus, live in a
former council house...

Under-valuing the family silver   ⟋ *Amersham*   *Over : Britoil.*
To float a new issue of shares requires the entrepreneurial skills of the
City's **merchant banks**. It is they who are employed by the government
to bring a publicly owned firm or corporation to the market – they must
commission advertisers to publicize the offer, negotiate with the **institutional investors** (e.g. pension funds, life assurance companies and unit
trusts) whose fund managers have millions of pounds at their disposal.
It is they who form the backbone of demand. Selling monoliths the size
of British Telecom and British Gas, with the assets of each valued at £8
billion, has set records for flotations. It is the merchant banks who
advise on the all-important offer-price for subscribers. To pitch the
price too low produces criticism of lost revenue. There have been some
bad misjudgements.

Amersham International, which until privatization was a virtually
unknown supplier of medical equipment, produced screaming head-
lines and a political furore. It was over-subscribed twenty times and
provoked charges of 'giving away state assets' to capitalists and 'selling
the country short'. But the French have done worse; their last three
privatizations averaged an over-subscription of fifty times each.

Britoil was an embarrassing flop when the sale of the first 51 per cent of the shares was attempted in 1982: more than two-thirds of the available shares were unsold. When the remaining 49 per cent were brought to the market in 1985, seven nervous merchant banks formed a syndicate to **underwrite** the offer (to guarantee to buy the shares as a last resort). This second issue was massively over-subscribed – as nearly all the flotations have been – and it compromised the much-publicized wider share-owning aspect of privatization. Only 12 per cent of the shares were available directly to the British public, 6 per cent were reserved for employees, 20 per cent were placed abroad. The rest – nearly two-thirds – went *under guarantee* to the City's institutional investors. In the harsh reality of the marketplace capitalism triumphs over idealism.

Yet in the political marketplace positive economics usually yields to the **'political utility function'**: governments maximize short-term political vote-catching returns at the expense of resource optimization. Throughout the 1980s the silver has been under-valued in an attempt to establish 'people's capitalism'.

How to turn silver to gold
'People's capitalism' is Mrs Thatcher's phrase for the irrepressible increase in small shareholders since 1979, and the privatization programme has been its driving force. A Treasury-commissioned survey for 1987 gave a figure of nearly 20 per cent of the adult population owning shares in publicly quoted companies: this should be compared with only 7 per cent in 1979. Eight per cent hold shares only in privatized companies. With over one million council houses sold since 1979 the aims of the Thatcher governments have been:

- a share-owning democracy;
- a property-owning democracy.

Both have blossomed on the rich soil of capital gain. Council houses have been sold at a fraction of their market value. Under-valued state silver has turned to gold as first-time buyers have gleefully discovered the meaning of *stagging* – buying a new issue to sell at a premium profit a few days later when the Stock Exchange quotes, for the first time, buying and selling prices for the new shares. British Telecom stags made an 80 per cent profit on Day One.

Let us suppose that your parents decided to invest modestly in each of a representative group of privatization issues, as they were brought to market. They started in 1980, and their aim was to 'play the market' until 1988 and then present you with the 'gold' on your 18th birthday.

Look at Table 5 to see what kind of gain you might consider so far: they
bought 100 shares in each of the eleven firms. Check today's newspaper
for current share prices. How well might you have done?

Table 5 How to turn silver into gold

Company	Sale price per share	Date	1987 value of new issue per share*	Sum invested
British Aerospace	150p	1981	639p	£150
Cable & Wireless	168p	1981	397p	£168
Amersham International	142p	1982	598p	£142
Britoil	100p	1982	292p	£100
Associated British Ports	112p	1983	527p	£112
Enterprise Oil	185p	1984	275p	£185
Jaguar	165p	1984	562p	£165
British Telecom	130p	1984	307p	£130
British Gas	50p	1986	112p	£ 50
British Airways	85p	1987	173p	£ 85
Rolls-Royce	85p	1987	142p	£ 85
Total				£1 372

* Valuations can be misleading. If the Stock Exchange is 'bullish' then share
prices rise; if it is 'bearish' there are more sellers than buyers, and so prices fall.
These figures are for a bullish market (14.5.87).

Who owns the silver?

The Trustee Savings Bank, better known as the TSB, was privatized in
1986. As the consequence of a legal ruling by the House of Lords,
however, the proceeds went *not* to the Treasury but to the TSB. This is
therefore difficult to categorize other than as a special case. It was so
over-subscribed that a lottery was used to identify the lucky two million
applicants for shares: 2½ million were unsuccessful, including this writer....

Because of under-pricing and over-subscription many of the privatizations have needed a scaling-down system of allocation: an individual who applied for 400 shares in Rolls-Royce, for example, received
only 150 (no prize for guessing the name of the individual...).

Sell the silver but keep the gold?

In publicizing its privatization schemes the Thatcher governments made
much of the popular belief that the legal transfer would end the meddle-
some interference of government ministers in the affairs of the former
state-owned firms and corporations. In some cases, however, the gov-

ernment holds a 'golden share' which gives it the exclusive right to veto any takeover which it would regard as not in the strategic interest of the country.

It is self-evident why it holds such shares in British Aerospace, Rolls-Royce and the Royal Ordnance. British Petroleum was a 51 per cent government shareholding whose origin could be traced back some decades; it was designed to stop BP falling into foreign ownership. With the advent of the Thatcher privatization period it was an early candidate, and parts of the government shareholding were sold when the market was buoyant (1979 and 1983). The government's remaining 32 per cent share – valued at £6 billion – was on course for another successful flotation when, in October 1987, the weakness of the US dollar caused a worldwide collapse in share prices. Given an interim offer price of 120p, which the pundits thought right, the Great Crash of 1987 caused the price to collapse to only 70p. Accordingly, the public did not buy and the underwriters had to instead. The Kuwaiti Investment Office moved quickly, and with surplus 'petrodollar' earnings bought 22 per cent of BP; one-fifth of BP is now in foreign ownership.

Meanwhile, when BP made a hostile takeover bid for the newly privatized Britoil, the government waived its right of veto with its 'golden share'. A different government might have acted differently.

Repairing the silver

When Rolls-Royce went bankrupt in 1971 it was nationalized – ironically – by the then Conservative government. This was justified on strategic grounds, to give it time to restructure – to bring the wounded patient back to full capitalist health and strength, able then to return to the private sector. The market in 1987 agreed, when Rolls-Royce shares were ten times over-subscribed with two million applicants. Ferranti, the defence electronics firm, also fits the category and was an early privatization success.

Antagonists of such *hospitalization* have scornfully remarked about 'lame ducks' – firms that have been rescued unjustifiably. Unless you live in either Oxford or Coventry you may well feel that the Rover Group, formerly British Leyland, qualifies for this label. It was never officially nationalized, but without massive injections of government cash over the years it would not have survived. To make Rover attractive enough for British Aerospace to buy it, the government wrote off £530m. worth of Rover debts in 1988.

A shrewd entrepreneur was appointed to the ailing Jaguar cars division of BL and told that if it could not be brought round to profitability quickly it would be closed. His success in its flotation in 1984 placed him in the millionaire listings. Jaguar shares boomed and the company recruited more labour for its expansion of output. In 1981 Jaguar made only 14 000 cars with 7 000 workers; in 1987 it produced 47 000 with 13 000 workers.

Polishing the silver

A successful privatization flotation requires a successful firm. The problem at British Airways was to turn the corporation back into profitability, after years of mismanagement and labour unrest. This was achieved by 1987 and again the shares were over-subscribed. British Aerospace was already profitable and its return to the private sector in 1981 was comparatively easy. The fact that firms and corporations need to be efficient and buoyant to make them successful candidates for flotation raises an interesting question. Our study of privatization in theory made much of public sector sub-optimization of resource use compared with the market disciplines of capitalism; so it is curiously ironic that these disciplines can persuade Jaguar, Ferranti, British Airways etc. into 'efficiency' *before* privatization. Evidently the simplistic divide

Public sector Inefficient
Private sector Efficient

argued by some of the enthusiasts is far from clear-cut. Privatization is supposed to deliver the goods. But the goods are delivered before privatization. Odd?

Employees' capitalism

The National Freight Corporation does not fit neat categorization because it was not brought to market in the sense used so far. Its managing director put together a financial package in 1982 which valued it at £100 million, and with bank loans its managers and 20 000 workers bought it out. An NFC employee who put £1 000 into his firm in 1982 would have five years later an asset valued at £46 000.

Employee share ownership on this scale makes NFC an interesting test-bed for industrial relations. It should be obvious to any worker that if his firm thrives then he will thrive, but this can be somewhat abstract in class-ridden Britain. For many workers the interpretation is that if the firm thrives then the already rich absentee shareholders get richer. **Industrial democracy** – the election of union representatives to management boards as 'worker directors' – was a panacea offered by the Left in the 1970s to improve industrial relations. Perhaps employees' capitalism will prove a superior alternative for the 1980s. Marx's proletariat,

proletariat → worker capitalists.

owning no capital and able to sell only their labour, are being turned
into capitalists by privatization; they are in a process of what is called
embourgeoisement by the French.

In 1979 there were only 30 employee-ownership schemes, but the
figure now is comfortably into four figures. The militant unions at
British Airways informed the company chairman that their compliance
in the 1987 privatization could be purchased – with a guarantee of a
substantial employee share option at favourable rates. Most of the
privatizations have followed this line. There are now 3½ million people
who hold shares in the company for which they work. The unions at
British Telecom opposed privatization, but now 96 per cent of the
workforce are shareholders.

To return to the restructuring of the Rover Group: Leyland Bus, a
loss-making subsidiary, has been sold to a consortium of its own
managers backed by a number of institutions. A management-led buy-
out for £50 million has given them a 75 per cent stake in Unipart,
Rover's spare-part subsidiary. The 4 000 employees will own 5 per cent
of the company.

Taking the family, with the silver, for a picnic
Rolls-Royce and British Airways have glamour because of what they do
or how they do it. In comparison there are some sectors of transport in
this country which can be regarded as fairly dull in comparison, until
1980 that is. Since the deregulation of express bus routes that year fares
have fallen 40 per cent and the quality of service improved with the
introduction of new vehicles. Buses that thunder past me on the motor-
ways advertise enticingly on the back:

> Hostess Service   Refreshments   Video   Reclining Seats
> Washroom   Toilets

which, with the sale of the motorway service centres, has also brought a
welcome improvement in quality of service. Shareholders in the newly
privatized Sealink cross-channel ferries might well consider investing in
the Channel Tunnel scheme, however.

No momentous changes have yet sprung from the 1985 Transport
Act. But, as so often, advances in technology can be the engine of
change, and the successful advent of the 'midi bus' in Exeter, which
seats 18 passengers, has more customer appeal than the traditional
gear-grinding municipal authority bus; it is also cheaper to run. This
should mean that the 1985 deregulation for towns will match that of the
1980 Act for express routes. Evidently the Scots are more enterprising
on this score, causing traffic congestion in Glasgow city centre as

private operators compete for business. One-third of the commercially registered buses around Edinburgh are in the private sector.

On unprofitable, but socially necessary, routes operators receive subsidies awarded on the basis of competitive tender. Refer back to Figure 18. Do you agree that a profit-maximizing bus operator, without a subsidy, would provide only OQ_a services, but, with a subsidy, can be induced to increase the quantity to OQ_b?

The natural monopolies

British Telecom plc

The deregulation of BT started in 1981 when it was separated from the Post Office and their statutory monopolies were withdrawn. BT plc dates from 1984. The removal of the statutory barrier to entry has given the Secretary of State for Industry power to license a rival, Mercury Communications. This new **duopolist** is able to confound the economics textbooks by capitalizing on electronic innovation. It is creating a rival network using optical fibre laid alongside British Rail track to connect the major cities, where it expects to be able to compete. According to economics texts telecommunications are a *public utility* so they appear on the list in Table 2: i.e. there can be only one supplier, a natural monopolist, with barrier to entry economies of scale. The consortium-owners of Mercury, who are Cable & Wireless, British Petroleum and Barclays Merchant Bank, are obviously convinced that the fledgling Mercury can upset the textbooks. If so, then the terminology will have to be changed to *natural duopoly*.

To do so it has required the establishment of the *Office of Telecommunications* (OFTEL) to police the industry and meet the criticism that privatization can merely substitute a private sector monopoly for a public sector one. Deregulation was necessary to move BT into the private sector, but a different kind is required to make it work in the public interest: regulation! If significant monopoly power remains then regulation and competition policy can be resorted to. Already OFTEL has ruled that Mercury must be allowed unlimited access to the BT network so that Mercury can connect to anyone in the country. Here again is a potential contestable market opportunity in which ownership of the grid could have been retained by the public sector, but this was not done.

BT announced record profits of £2 billion in 1987. Does BT have a licence to print money despite the OFTEL watchdog? Shackleton dismisses OFTEL as 'woefully inadequate'. Beesley and Littlechild are critical of 'government nannies'. Even so the influence of Professor

Littlechild can be seen in the regulations for both British Gas plc and British Telecom plc. They have been instructed by the Treasury to adopt his formula for price increases, so that

Increase $\leqslant$ **RPI minus** x.

RPI is the *Retail Price Index* to be used to measure the rate of inflation, and x has been set, initially, at 3 per cent. Hence neither may increase prices each year by more than 3 per cent below the rate of inflation. In this way it is hoped that these corporations will be forced to contain costs and not pass on inefficiency to their consumers with price increases. In 1988 the Director of OFTEL increased x to $4\frac{1}{2}\%$.

• One disgruntled subscriber is less than impressed with the service so far to judge from his irate letter to *The Times*, reproduced in Figure 20. When you have read through this refer back to question eight of the data response question in Chapter 1. What is the correlation?

British Gas Corporation plc

When offshore gas was discovered in the 1960s, British Gas was granted a legal **monopsony** – the right of first refusal in purchasing terms. This was withdrawn in 1982. BGC's monopoly in supplying gas to industry was broken in 1986, when onshore gas flowed to a brickworks from a private company. But a new pipeline had to be built from wellhead to factory.

When it was privatized in 1986, BGC was given a supervisory body **OFGAS**, an Office of Gas Supply under a Director General, to oversee gas prices and the terms and conditions of supply, and a Gas Users Council to handle complaints by consumers. Domestic gas consumers were given special opportunities to buy shares. The economic issues of pricing, competition and degree of regulation for this monopoly-buyer/ monopoly-seller, are enormously important.

British Gas has a complete monopoly of gas transmission and distribution. Transmission is a natural monopoly because of economies of scale and the investment waste of duplication of competing facilities. There is no reason, however, why British Gas should be the only user of the transmission lines. Legislation has been passed to allow competing firms to purchase its use for routing their gas. If the grid operated as a separate profit centre, the corporation could charge area boards as though they were outside customers. No British oil company has sold gas directly to industry as yet, from the North Sea fields; they cannot resolve the problem of cost of access to BGC's pipelines. This is clearly a

Two faces of Telecom

From Mr R. G. Selby-Boothroyd

Sir, I can confirm that at least one British Telecom employee would agree with Mr Engleheart (June 26) that the shareholders may grin while some of us bear it.

Last Saturday morning, a relative of mine attempted to discover, from an engineer at my local telephone exchange, why her attempts to dial my telephone number had continually resulted in the 'unobtainable tone'. She was told that the number had been disconnected because a bill had not been paid.

When she pointed out that the subscriber had not been living at the house long enough to have been presented with a bill, let alone long enough to have had the opportunity to default on payment, she was told that there was nothing that could be done until Monday morning.

When asked what kind of a service the engineer thought this represented, he replied: 'We're not here to give a service; we're here to make a profit for our shareholders.'

While British Telecom remains the only potential supplier of our telephone service, its shareholders can, presumably, continue to expect profits from the business of not giving the service.

Yours faithfully,
R. G. SELBY-BOOTHROYD,
63 Furlong Road,
Bourne End,
Buckinghamshire.
26 June 1985

Throughout 1987 and 1988 British Telecom has suffered a mounting barrage of criticism. Opinion polls have indicated growing dissatisfaction with BT's prices and standards of service. In the process it has given privatization a bad name. BT and BGC are held to be examples of how not to and why not to privatize.

OFTEL published details of a survey it carried out which found 23 per cent of call boxes out of order nationwide, rising to 38 per cent in London. One in six boxes were out of order for three consecutive weeks or more. Vandals, of course, are a national concern – BT has repaired 051 207 3106, in Everton, 40 times in nine months.

OFTEL has threatened BT with the introduction of competition. Mercury could be licensed to run its own call-boxes, or other businesses operate part of the existing service. Tough-minded regulation is beginning to benefit the consumer. BT accepts that the nationwide call-box fault figure must be down to 10 per cent by the end of 1988, and in 1989 it will have to make compensation payments to customers if, because of its own inefficiency, faults are not repaired within two days.

Figure 20

case where a contestable market was called for, but BG plc are using the grid as a barrier to entry.

These are considerable major issues which were aired by a writer of a letter to *The Times* (see Figure 21). There you read of the proposal that 'plans require major scrutiny and public debate ... examining alternative privatization schemes ...' This has not been the norm so far for any privatization: the government has not called for 'informal debate'.

A physical two-way link with the Continent seems essential for competition. As yet, British Gas cannot import, as electricity can, into the national grid. The conflict between government and private industry is neatly summed up in two decisions:

- The Ministry of Energy has vetoed the purchase of Norwegian gas.
- BGC was restructured; it was forced to surrender Enterprise Oil. The combative chairman of British Gas says that, now privatized, BG will move back into oil exploration because oil and gas go together.

Here are shades of the NEDO report: '... relationships between government and nationalized industries can have damaging economic consequences'.

Meanwhile British Gas, like BT, is coming under mounting public criticism (see Figure 22).

The welfare state

'Private Pensions plc'

This was the snappy label that the *New Statesman* produced for the proposed 1985 reform of the social security system. As we saw in Chapter 2, social security expenditure accounts for nearly 27 per cent of total public spending. The Minister for Health and Social Security introduced the reform with the criticism that the welfare state's transfer payment system is 'a leviathan with a life of its own'.

Much of the projected increase in its size was attributable to **SERPS**, the State Earnings-Related Pension Scheme, introduced by the previous Labour government, but with scant regard for the facts of basic **demography**. It had aimed to increase the real value of state pensions. Demographers calculate that when YOU will be retiring there will be 13 million pensioners instead of the 9 million now. Moreover, the ratio of working contributors paying for them through weekly national insurance payroll tax would fall from a current ratio of 2.5 down to only 1.5. In *New Statesman* language, the next century would face a pensions 'time bomb', a funding requirement of enormous size.

Pensioners ↑ another ratio ↓

The proposed reform was to shift the cost of the earnings-related part to the individual who would be induced to join a private pension plan to which the government and employer would also contribute, thus leaving the standard pension untouched. The founder of the welfare state, Lord Beveridge, did not, in his own provocative words, hang for what he had done. Forty years on he provided the opportunity for the minister seeking to reform it to hang instead, because the proposals stirred up violent criticism. The president of the Confederation of British Industry, the employers' association, told him that his proposals should be 'thrown on the bonfire'.

What he meant was that industry was fearful of an increase in labour costs. The government retreated: a slimline version of its part-privatized pensions plan commences in 1988; the voluntary private top-up part is very modest.

Case study: The National Health Service

Encouraged by the media, the public-opinion view is that the hospital sector of the NHS is in crisis because it is under-funded by the government. Certainly there is a crisis: wards are being closed, operations postponed and anguished nurses are striking. Cutting taxes in the Spring budget of 1988, the Chancellor was greeted by cries of 'Shame!' from the Opposition because the money did not go to the NHS instead. The public is now antagonistic to health privatization. What insight can positive economic analysis offer?

In its present form the NHS exists to provide health care to the 90 per cent of the population that demands it, free at the point of delivery. The other 10 per cent pay for health care. As a merit good the consumption of which the government wishes to encourage, this requires public sector funding for public sector provision. This is the basis of opposition to privatization: under-provision and inequitable consumption patterns could emerge in a market for health. Externality benefits would be reduced and NHS economies of scale lost. Harley Street offers cosmetic surgery to ageing soap opera stars, it is not interested in paupers. Refresh your memory of the *laissez faire* economy described in Chapter 2.

There is then a demand curve for health which is not perfectly inelastic. In Figure 23, if there is zero price then over-consumption is implied. If the NHS charged price P instead, then demand would fall from OQ_1 to OQ_2. But, as the product is not homogeneous, how is the utility of a facial wart removal to be measured – as cosmetic or caring surgery? Do you recall the three 'efficiency criteria' in the cartoon in Chapter 3? How sympathetic to maximizing patient throughput (pro-

Need for rethink on gas privatization

From Mr Allan Sykes

Sir, In your July 2 second leader you urge the need for avoiding a monolithic coal industry in isolation from customers and markets. You stress that the wider national interest requires the industry to be split and run efficiently and competitively. Precisely the same reasoning should apply to the privatization of the British Gas Corporation (BGC), but this is not the Government's intention.

The oil industry are worried about present plans, but they are inhibited from speaking out themselves for two reasons: first, the BGC looks like remaining the sole purchaser for their gas; second, the sponsoring privatization ministry, the Department of Energy (DEn), is also the oil and gas-exploration licensing authority. As such licences are the lifeblood of oil companies they are ill-placed to dispute public policy matters in their industry. It is thus important for others to air all the major issues now while time permits.

The general case for privatisation is that it raises efficiency by increasing the importance of market forces at the expense of political and bureaucratic influences. The more a nationalised industry is sensibly capable of being broken up the greater the likely gains in efficiency from the benefits of decentralised decision-taking and competition.

Breaking up the BGC into, say, regional units will not make distribution, an inseparable monopoly activity, competitive. It will, however, permit efficiency comparisons and cause welcome competition in the development of more efficient marketing policies and in the purchase of gas.

The monopoly buying rights of the BGC largely destroyed the incentive for gas exploration in British waters between the late 1960s and early 1980s to the clear detriment of the British economy, export earnings and jobs. That should not be allowed to happen again. Gas purchasing should be split between regional gas authorities and oil companies should be free to export gas.

It must be seriously doubted if the DEn or anyone else could produce any regulatory scheme as efficacious as allowing competitive forces in a multi-unit industry. Further, the initial regulatory system can never be significantly amended.

The prospectus for the estimated, £8 billion flotation must clearly state the regulatory system. No important amendment could occur without protest and probably litigation. Investors could justifiably claim they would not have paid so much in the light of such amendment. Hence the initial regulatory system must be virtually perfect. Any serious error could be rectified only by nationalisation, hardly a reassuring prospect for a Conservative Government.

The creation overnight of an £8 billion corporation, i.e., nearly the size of BP, restrained only by a 'simple' regulatory system would represent an undesirable concentration of economic power. Such a BGC could grow much bigger still by becoming a major oil producer in its own right by acquisition, and also by demanding a major share in oil company exploration programmes as the price of future gas-purchase contracts. A large new oil company which is also a private gas monopoly is inherently undesirable.

The proposed BGC privatisation plans require major scrutiny and public debate if damaging mistakes are not to occur. The Government should amend its plans, publish a Green Paper examining alternative privatisation schemes, and allow time for informed debate on the significant issues involved. Any delay in the receipt of £8 billion will be more than offset by the national gains from increased competition and efficiency.

Yours faithfully,
ALLEN SYKES,
Mallington,
The Mount,
Leatherhead,
Surrey.
3 July 1985

(Reproduced by permission of The Times Newspapers Ltd)

Questions:

1. What word would you use to replace the writer's word 'monolithic'?
2. The oil industry was reluctant to speak out because BGC is the sole purchaser of gas. Economists' word for sole purchaser? Significance?
3. How would breaking up the BGC into regional units help the national interest?
4. Why is contestable market theory relevant to this industry?
5. What foregone 'aggregate net benefits' (see page 46) are outlined here?
6. Why does the writer regard regulation as a second-best solution?
7. What is a Green Paper and what are its claimed advantages?

Figure 21

Monopoly row sparked by 6% gas price rise

BRITISH GAS is raising charges for its 16.5 million domestic customers by an average of 6 per cent from the beginning of April in a move which is bound to provoke a fresh row about the powers of privatised monopolies.

Consumer groups and opposition leaders yesterday condemned the increases, which are 2.7 percentage points above the present rate of inflation, and come only days after price rises averaging 9 per cent were confirmed by electricity boards.

Ian Powe, director of the Gas Consumers' Council, said he was 'shocked by this completely unexpected announcement'.

'It is stretching the credibility of the public to the limit. British Gas could not have done this if it operated as it should do in a competitive environment rather than as a monopoly,' Mr Powe said.

Ofgas, the Government-sponsored watchdog set up to protect the interests of gas consumers, said the price increases would be scrutinised closely to check that they complied with the terms of privatisation.

British Gas has faced mounting criticism over the past year over alleged abuse of its monopoly position while the regulatory regime under which the company was privatised has been widely condemned as far too lax.

Jeremy Warner
Business Correspondent

Figure 22 From *The Independent*, 19 March 1988

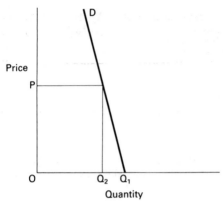

Figure 23 Health care demand

ductivity) is a bedridden post-operation consumer of health care?

Turn now to Figure 24. What is the OECD average? How does Britain compare? Only six countries out of the 24 spend less. But a word of caution: GDP comparisons do not allow for different standards of living. Richer countries spend more on health care than poorer ones.

To overcome this use Table 6. Assuming that France and Germany are 'similar' countries to our own, are the expenditures similar? If public expenditure on health in the UK matched the OECD average, then the Chancellor in his 1988 Spring budget would have needed to put a further £2 billion into the NHS. He had this available from selling the

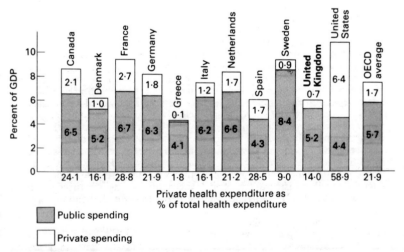

Figure 24 Health spending as a percentage of GDP (1985)

family silver. Instead he balanced the budget as well as reducing income tax. Would £2 billion have produced a better health service? The answer is surprising: we do not know.

There is little evidence that higher spending automatically guarantees a better health service. Economic theory offers the concept of the return on one extra £ spent. Applied economics cannot deliver this, despite the impressive technical language in the cartoon – 'productivity, cash flow and cost–benefit analysis'. The Centre for Health Economics at the University of York has calculated 'death rate indicators': you are seven times more likely to survive an operation in Harrow than in Grimsby. The DHSS is trying to introduce 'performance indicators' to make inter-hospital comparisons.

Table 6 Total health expenditure
(US $ per head 1985)

United States	1 776
Canada	1 282
Sweden	1 172
France	1 072
Germany	983
Netherlands	938
Denmark	755
Italy	678
United Kingdom	*627*
Spain	456
Greece	252
OECD average	848

An extra £2 billion spent on the NHS could all go into pay increases for doctors and nurses. This would get public approval; it would not reopen wards or reduce queues for operations (details on page 30).

Guys Hospital in London is run, within budget, by its clinicians: they decide its medical priorities. The claim is that the hospital is cleaner and provides a better service. Its Director of Surgery blames NHS problems on what he calls 'deficiency disease'. By this he means the poor skills of hospital administrators – if they run over budget they postpone operations to save money, they do not reduce jobs for administrators. Perhaps an economist's diagnosis would be monopoly 'X-inefficiency' disease?

In peripheral activities better management of resources has been achieved by contracting out laundry, cleaning and meals services. Public provision and public production has been replaced by public provi-

sion and private production. In the definition in Figure 1 this was called
... what? NHS hospitals could do this for medical services, too, by
buying certain expertise from the private hospitals and specializing on
the others. As for schools (page 49), so NHS hospitals could compete
for patients.

The issues raised over privatizing the health service range through
efficiency, both productive (individual hospitals) and allocative (consumer choice and range of facilities) and equity considerations. Geriatic
hospitals and hospitals for the mentally ill cannot be seen to fit into a
market mechanism. Would the poor be disadvantaged with second-
class care? There are redistribution of income elements if taxes are
lowered and customers expected to pay for medical insurance. For 90
per cent of the population the state acts paternalistically; for the future
it looks as if it will continue to do so. To reassure voters in the 1987
election Mrs Thatcher was forced into declaring 'The National Health
Service is safe with us'.

All is far from plain sailing for the privatizing government even on its
own doorstep. The all-party Social Services Committee of the House of
Commons has criticized the privatization programme for hospital
cleaning, laundry and catering because it has saved only 1 per cent of its
normal costs. This seems to ignore some basic features of economics,
including the importance not just of cost but also of quality. The
criticism of the MPs that so far the scheme 'has not brought home the
bacon' ignores – in the case of hospital catering – that the bacon needs
to be varied, hot and reliable.

A wider definition of privatization

Rolling back the frontier of the public sector can take a number of forms
and bring a variety of gains. The recent tender to London Transport for
52 routes is designed to save money: were it to fall short the Commons
Committee would, no doubt, be critical – in which case they might put
their minds to consider such non-price consumer gains as punctuality,
cleanliness and reliability.

Privatization has a, wide range in its coverage and a wide range of
possible benefits when the frontier of the public sector is rolled back and
the frontier of the private sector rolled forward. The sections which
follow are a summary of this wider definition and the specific forms it
has taken so far.

1. Public flotations
Refer back to Table 1.

2. *Private flotations, bought by other companies, or management buy-out*

		£m
National Freight Corporation	1984	5
British Rail Hotels	1983	45
Jaguar (British Leyland)	1984	297
Sealink (British Rail)	1984	66
Johnson Matthey Bank	1984	40
British Shipbuilders warship yards (Yarrow & Vosper)	1985	54
British Airways Helicopters	1986	13
Unipart (Rover Group)	1987	52
Leyland Bus (...)	1987	4
Leyland Trucks (...)	1987	0
Royal Ordnance	1987	190
BR Wagon Works	1987	6
Rover Group	1988	150
British Shipbuilders Govan Yard	1988	6

Revenue from sales paid to holding company, *not* the Treasury.

3. *Joint ventures*
No statistics available for these joint public and private sector ventures.

4. *Deregulation*
- National Bus Company monopoly on express routes ended.
- BT monopoly of telephone handsets removed.
- Mercury Communications established to break BT monopoly.
- Electricity: private power-stations legalized and grid monopoly ended.
- Gas: private production legalized and grid monopoly ended.

5. *The welfare state*
- Contracting out (franchising) for private provision of hospital laundry, catering and cleaning.
- SERPS modified and private top-up pension plans encouraged from 1988 onwards.
- Sale of council houses: the 'Right to Buy' programme. Proceeds to local councils. Dates and amounts (£ million):

1979–80	80–81	81–82	82–83	83–84	84–85	85–86	86–87
494	698.5	1 390.2	1 983.3	1 524.6	1 300.3	1 253	1 535.1

6. Future proposals

- Private sector landlords for council tenants in Housing Association Trusts.
- Compulsory tendering by all councils for hospital services, plus extension to school meals, vehicle maintenance, administration of leisure centres.
- Education: 25 City Technical Colleges are to be set up by private funds, but the running costs will be set by central government.

The above are in addition to more of the same – further sales of nationalized industries will take place as and when they look suitable for a successful share flotation.

Key facts
Since 1979:

- Home owners have increased from 52 to 66 per cent of the population.
- Share owners have increased from 7 to 20 per cent.
- 30 per cent of people were classified as middle class, now it is 40 per cent.

KEY WORDS

Merchant banks	OFTEL
Institutional investors	RPI minus x formula
Underwrite	Monopsony
Political utility function	OFGAS
Industrial democracy	SERPS
Duopolist	Demography

Reading list
Barr, 'The pensions time bomb', *Economic Review*, vol. 2, Sept. 1984.
Littlechild, 'Deregulation of UK telecommunications', *Economic Review*, vol. 1, Nov. 1983.
Le Grand, 'Survival of the welfare state', *Economic Review*, vol. 5, Nov. 1987.

Essay topics
1. Define privatization. Is it a mixed blessing?
2. The chairman of the nationalized British Gas Corporation opposed

privatization of his industry; he did not think it appropriate. Was he right?

3. 'Post-privatization the RPI minus x formula will be the consumers' salvation'. Will it?

Data response question 5
BT improves by 12 per cent

Answer the following questions based on the accompanying article, which is taken from the *Financial Times* of 19 June 1987.

1. BT's profits are here the accounting profession's calculations. How do economists differ from businessmen in their concept of profit?
2. Post-privatization BT makes the PSBR lower. How? (2 reasons)
3. What is the price regulation formula imposed on the private BT by the government? It endeavours to achieve what in economic terms?
4. The major expenditure item on capital account for BT in the 1980s is to switch over to digital technology. What consumer benefits would justify this?
5. Would a profit-maximizing private sector monopolist calculate the full economic costs and returns on rural telephone kiosks? If so, what would be the conclusion?
6. How has the demand for domestic calls changed during 1986/87? Draw a diagram to illustrate this change.
7. How has the demand for labour by BT changed during 1986/87? Draw a diagram to illustrate this change.
8. Why has BT changed its industrial relations policy?
9. Does BT have a 'licence to print money'?

BT improves by 12% to £2.07bn

SIR GEORGE JEFFERSON, chairman of British Telecommunications, yesterday revealed that profits for the 1986–87 year had surged to £2.07bn at the pre-tax level.

That was an improvement of 11.7 per cent over the previous year's £1.85bn and bang on the figure anticipated by City analysts.

The final quarter contribution also improved by 11.7 per cent to £555m. Sir George said the overall effect on profits of the two-and-a-half week industrial action by staff during the quarter was not material with lower revenues being roughly matched by lower operating costs.

However, the dispute did prompt the directors to omit payment of the employee profit sharing scheme this time – in 1985–86 employees shared £18m.

Turnover for the full year to end-March improved from £8.39bn to £9.42bn with the fourth quarter tally of £2.42bn showing an increase of 8.4 per cent.

One of the main reasons for the improvement in sales was strong growth in rentals of business lines and private circuits, particularly in the City.

Operating profits for 1986–87 increased from £2.12m to £2.35m. Pre-tax profits were struck after deducting net interest charges of £282m (£267m) – last year's profits were before the employee profit sharing allocation.

Tax accounted for £754m (£743m) to leave earnings per 25p share 3.8p higher at 20.9p.

A final dividend of 5.1p raises the total from 7.5p to 8.45p net.

During 1986–87 the volume of domestic calls went up by 7 per cent and those for international traffic by 11 per cent.

The year saw a 4,800 reduction in staff. A further decline of some 5,000 is forecast for this year with a bigger acceleration as modernisation comes through.

Investment in new plant and equipment exceeded £2bn for the first time. The figure should increase in the current year as Sir George was not expecting a slow-down in the rate of installation of digital exchanges.

The chairman noted that the board recognised the challenge of meeting the growing needs and expectations of customers in an increasingly competitive and demanding environment.

He said in meeting that challenge BT intended to build on the success it had already achieved and also expand the new directions in which it had started to move.

Chapter Six
Privatization and the public sector

'The virtues and defects of privatization are to be found in the eye of the beholder.' Peacock

The New Enlightenment

In the eighteenth century the Enlightenment was an explosion of liberty of ideas which questioned prejudices and superstitions. In the last quarter of the twentieth century the willingness to question the economic rationale of the public sector, its size and constituent parts, could be deemed to be a New Enlightenment (a phrase borrowed from Graham and Clarke – see the reading list).

The old microeconomics can be summarized as: market failures justify a role of intervention by governments. The new microeconomics is: government failures justify a role for markets.

It is reported that the British Treasury has been approached by many governments seeking details of the mechanics of privatization. Even the Japanese government is selling its share of Nippon Telegraph and Telephone. And yet here in Britain, for none of its privatization schemes did the government offer an analysis of aggregate net benefits prior to legislation.

The supply side reform of extensive privatization, a radically innovative economic policy for this country, is aimed at increasing allocative and productive efficiency. If this form of industrial policy is successful then the performance of the British economy will improve. Having suffered the ignominy of being labelled the sick man of Europe by our EEC partners – poor at economic growth, notorious for strikes and sour industrial relations, superseded by formerly poorer countries that have now a higher per capita standard of living, always suffering a higher rate of inflation and lower productivity growth than the average – the 1980s have witnessed something of a rejuvenation.

There is no definite way of proving that the economic reforms of the 1980s have encouraged growth. Yet recently Britain has led the EEC in its annual percentage change of GDP, instead of trailing in the rear. Trades union reforms have reduced strikes, financial deregulation has intensified competition between banks and building societies, industrial productivity has risen dramatically, and privatization has produced better business practices. At this early stage in its history the virtues and defects of privatization may well be found in the eye (mind?) of the beholder, but let us see if economics can offer some guidance. In so doing, we shall then realize that its influence has reached the industries that have not been privatized – the remaining nationalized industries and the welfare state: privatization and the public sector are intimately interconnected. But first, the direct consequences of privatization so far.

Microeconomic aspects of privatization

Welfare gains in efficiency

In an economic environment of decision-making for want satisfaction, a *'first best'* solution would be if consumer sovereignty existed in its purest form. The competitive ideal of price equal to marginal cost supposes perfect knowledge, no externalities and perfect factor mobility.

In the economics of the real world the supporters of privatization argue for a *second best* solution as being a realistic aim because achieving it would be a definite improvement on the *third best* inefficiencies of the public sector. What is the evidence?

The gains in allocative efficiency are proved by the fall in prices and rise in quality for long-distance bus travellers. Productive efficiency has been achieved by Jaguar and the National Freight Corporation. Because of competition BP, British Aerospace, Rolls-Royce and Cable & Wireless were already efficient before privatization. There was no obvious reason why they should have remained partly or wholly owned by the state. The restructuring at Rover Group with the sale of Unipart, Leyland Bus, Leyland Trucks and the merger of Leyland Commercial Vehicles with Daf of Holland, may be the start of efficiency gains which would justify the return of Rover to the private sector as a former, wounded hero.

At the time of writing (Spring 1988) British Aerospace, itself recently privatized, has made a direct bid for Rover, to take it over.

Job creation

Direct job creation in the privatized sector has been limited: Jaguar has recruited an extra 1 000 operatives because of the success of its new models. For the most part the firms and industries involved have shed jobs before flotation, under pressure to make a success of their launch. The trade unions in telecommunications opposed privatization fearing that a private sector British Telecom would be more cost-conscious and efficiency-motivated than a public sector BT.

They were correct. Their 1987 pay claim was turned down and made conditional on a reduction of labour restrictive practices; the unions fought this and lost. The BT of the 1970s with a monopoly, in an expanding market, was a recruiter of labour. The privatized BT of the 1980s, facing a fledgling Mercury which has aggressively announced prices 20 per cent below those of BT, has forced BT to become a shedder of jobs. Thus far, with the exception of Jaguar, privatization seems to be a recipe for lengthening dole queues. Not so.

More efficient privatized firms create jobs in supplier industries as the privatized firms expand sales. More motor cars made means a rise in demand for headlights, leather upholstery, walnut fascias etc. More efficient, labour-shedding firms, after privatization, create jobs in other sectors of the economy if they reduce their prices, and these are important inputs for other firms: cheaper gas and telephones means lower costs for British industry. Privatization becomes the begetter of longer term hidden employment even though it may create direct unemployment in the short run.

Investment appraisal and efficiency

In Chapter 3 we studied the investment policy in the 1978 White Paper on the nationalized industries, which imposed an obligation on the NIs to seek to prove to the Treasury that a *required rate of return* on capital projects could justify the spending of public money. In an otherwise sympathetic report, the Monopolies and Mergers Commission's efficiency audit of the electricity industry in 1982 was critical of its investment appraisal which had failed to estimate demand trends and produced an industry with over-capacity.

A privatized corporation has to borrow in a commercial capital market such as the City or abroad; the Exchequer is relieved of the necessity to produce the funds. The privatized borrower has to conform to the private sector capital investment criteria which are more stringent than those of the Treasury, however much the Treasury would wish to simulate such a market. The factors of production – the nation's resources – are the crucial inputs in the supply equation of firms, which, if misallocated, cause waste and sub-optimal efficiency. In order to gain public sympathy, privatizing governments stress direct consumer benefits of their programmes; economists seek also the less direct but equally important 'hidden' gains. It is easy to see that breaking a monopoly and exposing a corporation to competition (e.g. Mercury Communications challenging British Telecom) is a consumer benefit. Consumers will also gain, however, when BT has to compete in the capital markets for the funds it will require to develop its telecommunications equipment.

Managerial buy-outs

The much-publicized National Freight Corporation buy-out by its managers and employees, with its attendant spectacular rises in value of asset holdings and gains in profitability and productivity, has made a major contribution in changing the climate of opinion. Entrepreneurs at Rover Group have followed this lead and bought out Unipart and Leyland Bus. Within the private sector Barclays Bank has seized the opportunity to make itself a buy-out financier with its Barclays Development Capital.

Figure 25 emphasizes the accelerating trend since 1979, within the economy as a whole. This particular form of privatization has started a trend which promises better firms, more motivated entrepreneurs and a growing wave of enterprise. A failure rate so far of only 10 per cent is remarkably low.

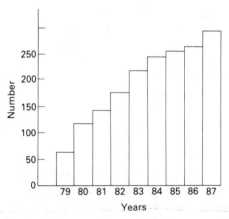

Figure 25   The trend in management buy-outs

Entrepreneurs and dynamic efficiency

Freed from the 'dead hand of Whitehall' and the interference of government ministers, entrepreneurs are likely to take the view that privatized firms will operate like the rest of the private sector and so offer the business opportunities that enterprising managers seek along with the rewards – higher incomes, job satisfaction, prestige and power which the public sector cannot produce. If better calibre management is an outcome of privatization, then the productive and allocative efficiency gains hoped for may become a reality.

A word or two of caution. Entrepreneurs are a standard feature of all economic textbooks. It may be that Britain's economic problem is too limited a pool of able entrepreneurs. It has needed a South African, Sir Michael Edwardes, to restructure BL; an Australian, Mr Rupert Murdoch, to rescue *The Times*, and an American-based Scotsman, Sir Ian McGregor, to restructure the steel industry and then coal. Is there sufficient managerial talent in Britain to cope with privatization? BT could overstretch itself and falter. Most of you are conversant with the BBC microcomputer – are you aware that in moving into the US market its manufacturer, Acorn, made a gross entrepreneurial blunder which brought the company to its knees: it had to be rescued by Olivetti. Because of its monolithic powers BT is supposed to have a licence to print money – but it could print $\frac{1}{2}$-pence pieces or £1 notes....

Natural monopolies and efficiency

Former state monopolies require *contestable markets* to force down costs; free entry and *exit* that is frictionless so the monopolist cost-minimizes to prevent competition starting up. Moreover, only *normal profits* will deter potential rivals. To be costless would require the sunk costs of the no-alternative-use capital – electricity grid, gas grid, water pipelines – to be state-owned. Enfranchised firms then hire their use. The exit costs of these firms would be low. Monopoly profit would disappear through potential, rather than realized, competition.

In Chapter 4 prominence was given to five industries for which the net consumer benefits could be greatest. Of these BT is already privatized; but a new entrant, Mercury Communications, was encouraged to provide competition, in preference to the market outlined above. The other four could fit this market: generating electricity at a privatized power station to feed into the (publicly owned) grid creates competition between these suppliers, there are low-cost power stations on low-cost coalfields and higher-cost units on less-efficient sites. The Post Office, British Rail and especially British Coal can be split into competing privatized units.

That the government chose to privatize the British Gas Corporation as a monopoly is a cause for concern; floating a monopoly on the stock market is easier and financially more rewarding for the seller than to devise a competitive alternative. Since the privatization of BGC, Sheffield Forgemasters – one of Britain's largest users of gas with an annual bill of £6 million – has had to switch to using liquified petroleum gas negotiated on a 10-year contract with a leading oil company, which will undercut BGC by 30 per cent in pricing. This looks like healthy competition: in fact it is the culmination of a long-running dispute with the monopolist that has provoked Sheffield Forgemasters to formally complain to the Monopolies Commission, the Office of Fair Trading and the EEC under Article 86 of the Treaty of Rome. The complaints allege unfair pricing policy, anti-competitive practices and destabilizing negotiating techniques.

Now turn back to Figure 20. Does the letter writer's relative have this kind of muscle to confront a monopoly Goliath? Consumer David is only successful if he has (competition?) pebbles for his sling.

It remains to be seen whether the Office of Gas will determine the tariffs if BGC tries to discriminate unfairly, whether it will monitor efficiency, rule on standards of service, arbitrate customer complaints, prescribe methods of comprehensible accounting so that BGC policies are understood, rather than deliberately obscured. An optimist could argue that even if mistakes were made in the format of privatization, subsequent pragmatic reforms can be imposed by the government to try to rescue the situation. We shall see. A profit-seeking private sector monopolist does not look like an obvious consumer benefit unless subject to tough regulation, American style. OFTEL is revealing itself as a force to be reckoned with; is OFGAS going to be equally as effective?

The problem is best summed up by a quotation from Davis and Davis: 'The new theory (contestable markets) gives a large green light to market forces, it gives a cautionary amber to privatization – indeed to some forms it authoritatively offers a glaring red' (see the reading list in Chapter 4).

Trade unions and productive efficiency
In so far as the trade unions feature in the consequences of privatization they do so in relation to the former nationalized industries rather than firms. The unions have, over the years, established themselves strongly in the public sector where the absence of the profit motive, shareholders, stock market ratings and market pressures have weakened management power in collective bargaining and correspondingly strengthened that of the unions. Large pay claims have been more readily conceded in the public sector, and restrictive labour practices, which protect overmanning, are strongly entrenched.

Many trade union officials who, by their nature, tend to be political activists, oppose privatization on principle and because they see their power-base threatened by the need for privatized industries to be profitable. The BT engineers went on strike to try to stop privatization but realized opposition was ineffective. The first strike after privatization, in 1987, was a victory for BT. Challenged to offer a double-figure pay increase without strings, it refused, insisting instead on the reduction of restrictive practices to increase efficiency; and with the productivity gain conceded the pay increase. The strike petered out and BT was the winner.

Supply-side reforms can be explicit (e.g. the labour market reforms designed to reduce the monopoly power of unions). Privatization is a supply-side reform by stealth if it also achieves this outcome. Little wonder that the Post Office unions are vehemently opposing privatization plans: they are aware of the productive efficiency gains that PO plc would force though.

Competition policy

Privatization gets a green light when it exposes former public sector activities to competitive market forces. The formal meaning of 'competition policy' is the legislation from 1948 to 1980 and the investigatory bodies it has created – the Office of Fair Trading, Monopolies and Mergers Commission and the Restrictive Practices Court – which have been instructed to further the public interest by seeking out anticompetitive practices and subjecting enterprises to efficiency audits. Privatization is, in theory, a form of competition policy. The formal structure, embodied in Acts of Parliament, is beginning to look in need of overhaul. The creation of OFGAS and OFTEL as separate supervisory entities adds to the bodies created by law, but the boundaries of responsibility are beginning to blur between them. The thrusting of so many firms and industries into the private sector looks to be producing a queue for the Monopolies and Mergers Commission to monitor. It and competition policy look in need of an overhaul. The extension of the privatization programme ought to hasten this. The present Director General of Fair Trading is firmly of the opinion that 'a radical reappraisal rather than minor amendment' is required to the legislation. Perhaps contestability rather than concentration should be the yardstick?

Wider share ownership

Privatization has come at the right time to complement the deregulation of the Stock Exchange in 1986 and the advances in communications technology. The fierce competition in the financial sector means that high street banks and shops will offer shares to buy over the counter. This breaks down socio-economic barriers. In his budget speech of 1988 the Chancellor of the Exchequer remarked: '... the emergence of the capital-owning democracy is one of the most remarkable features of the 1980s'.

Macroeconomic aspects of privatization

Fiscal policy

One reason for rolling back the frontier of the public sector has been the belief that it would produce lower taxes on incomes. The proceeds from the sale of the family silver allowed 2p reductions in income tax in the Spring Budgets of 1987 and 1988; further cuts are promised. Some critics regard this as subsidizing a riotous living because real incomes have been rising anyway. A supply-side reformer would point to the incentive effect of lower taxes; a critic would wonder why the 'privatization swag' could not have been put back into state-funded capital projects – new hospitals, schools and prisons, for example. The local authorities were given the choice of spending income from the sale of council houses on either reducing debt or building more houses. Central government chose a different path: the nation's stock of capital changed owners but did not increase in volume.

The public sector borrowing requirement

The PSBR is the shortfall of the public sector in receipts compared with expenditure. Turn back to Figure 2 where we studied where the money comes from and where it goes. Notice now the bottom item on the left. The Bank of England, the government's bank, is responsible for borrowing. The problems that are produced are threefold: firstly, how the funding should be carried out; secondly, if it is a large sum, the fear of excessively high interest rates, themselves regarded as a restraint on business expansion because of the prohibitive cost of loans; and more recently a third problem has received a lot of attention – anxiety over crowding out. We now consider each in turn.

To fund the PSBR the Bank of England can print more money or it can persuade the public to buy gilt-edged securities, national savings certificates and premium bonds, all of which are instruments for lending to the public sector. For the lender the rate of interest is the attraction, even if, on premium bonds, this is disguised as a 'prize'.

The privatizing governments of the first half of the 1980s, believing that excessive money supply growth can be inflationary, introduced a **medium-term financial strategy** in 1980 which entailed a reduction in public expenditure coupled with specific money supply growth targets. To achieve these aims a reduction in the PSBR was essential. The large sums raised each year from privatization have been used to reduce the PSBR, cut taxes and maintain public expenditure at a higher level than it would have been otherwise. Using privatization money in these ways has provoked the criticism of 'subsidizing a riotous living'.

Crowding out

On the Stock Exchange, on an average day, three-quarters of any turnover is in government gilt-edged securities. It is thought that when there is a large PSBR and governments force up interest rates to sell the gilts to fund it, then this diverts essential funds away from private sector firms seeking financial capital for expansion. This is financial crowding out.

In so far as the City has shown an insatiable appetite for the privatization equity shares, then, when the natural monopolies are marketed, the flow of money into them is so great that some private sector firms may find it difficult to float a rival new issue at the same time. This is crowding out.

Firms that turn instead to bank loans increase the money supply. If there are money supply growth targets these are put under pressure and may be breached.

Sterling and the balance of payments

Neither of these is immune from the privatization programme. Some of the demand for shares has come from abroad, on a large scale. The Japanese are said to hold 8 per cent of British Gas shares. The accusation of 'selling the family silver' got a rough ride in Chapter 1; but it is true that, as non-residents are not part of the family, dividends paid to them in subsequent years out of profits will constitute a debit outflow item on the *interest, profit and dividends* part of the **invisibles account** (services) of the balance of payments.

Each time there is a large flotation of a state enterprise and heavy inflows of foreign funds seeking shares, the demand for sterling – the British £ sold on the foreign exchange market, which is said to be 'floating' because its daily **spot price** is determined by demand and supply – rises and so its price appreciates upwards. Because the price of sterling has a critical influence on the price of our exports and imports, the Bank of England may have an exchange rate policy which commits it to intervene (by becoming a buyer or seller) to stabilize the price. When the demand for sterling is heavy and the Bank sells, it loses control of the domestic money supply as new £s flood in.

Nationalized industries

The up-to-date list of NIs has taken on a shrunken appearance in comparison with its 1979 counterpart. Sixteen major state-owned companies have been transferred to the private sector. I have decided on three categories to fit the information known at the time of writing.

- *To be privatized:* water (England and Wales) and electricity (England, Wales and Northern Ireland), British Steel and National Giro Bank
- *Likely to be privatized:* Post Office, British Coal, Short Bros. (Belfast) and Harland & Wolff Shipyard (Belfast)
- *Others:* British Rail, British Shipbuilders, London Regional Transport, Civil Aviation Authority and British Waterways

Comparative data

In 1979 the NIs produced 10 per cent of UK output, 14 per cent of fixed investment and employed two million people.

In 1987 the corresponding figures were 5½ per cent, 9 per cent and 800 000 people.

Performance analysis

Having been instructed in the 1978 White Paper to contribute to economic welfare by being cost-efficient and achieve a stated return on capital employed, how well have the remaining NIs performed?

Molyneux and Thompson posed the rather pugnacious question: 'Nationalized industry performance: still third rate?' (consult the reading list), to which the answer would appear to be 'no longer'. This original accusation was based on a comparison of public and private enterprise which sought to 'prove' that private is economically preferable because it is more efficient.

Since 1979 there has been a striking improvement in many aspects of nationalized industries' performance. Gains in labour productivity have helped to cut costs substantially. After the 1970s decade of 'mutual recrimination' (see page 38) the 1980s have produced higher standards of management and efficiency with more effective financial control. Big improvements were made at the Post Office after the Monopolies and Mergers Commission criticized it for knowing little about its cost structures.

The correlation between employment and productivity is that, as in private manufacturing, there has been a sharp reduction in labour employment. The growth of the NIs' labour productivity has averaged 7 per cent a year over the four years to 1987 (compare the trends on Figures 26 and 27). This has been brought about by adding enormous numbers of steel workers and coal miners to the dole queue:

- British Steel: 1979 labour force 167 000; 52 000 in 1987
- British Coal: 1979 labour force 220 000 (225 pits open); 90 000 (96 pits open) in 1987

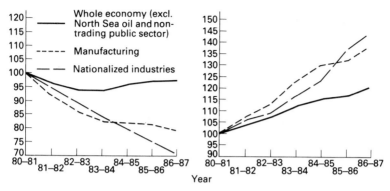

Figure 26 Employment   **Figure 27** Productivity

To set against these figures it is worth noting that the profitability of the NIs is still, generally, well below that of private industry in terms of real rate of return on capital. Some of the industries are suffering declining demand. Can you name five from the list? The average growth rate of output of only 1 per cent since 1983 – a period of prolonged expansion in the economy – is well below that of either private manufacturing or the economy as a whole.

That said, the most revealing comment on NI performance comes from the official mouthpiece of the Treasury, *Economic Progress Report* for December 1987 (from which Figures 26 and 27 are copied), which states:

> 'Industries facing privatization have been impelled by the prospect to increase efficiency. Even those expecting to remain in the public sector indefinitely have been stimulated by the example set by the privatized businesses.'

This seems to be a statement that comes very close to admitting that privatization is *not* necessary to achieve greater efficiency in resource use!

The privatization plans for electricity rest on splitting the generation side into two competing companies: a 'Big G' which will be 70 per cent of capacity, including all the nuclear stations, and a 'Little G' of 30 per cent. The twelve Area Boards having been sold separately, these will then jointly own the distribution grid. They will be under an obligation to buy 20 per cent of their electricity from the high-cost nuclear stations. There will be hidden deregulation for the coal industry; freed from the obligation to buy British coal, the generators could turn to cheaper imports. This seems to be a form of 'privatization' by stealth for still nationalized British Coal.

Conclusions

Privatization is one of the central economic policies of the decade. It is unquestionably controversial. The first data response exercise at the beginning of this book was a normative attack with an explicit title: 'The consumer is the loser'. It is to be hoped that what you have read in the subsequent chapters you have found to be rather more positive in approach! However, the core question from that critically expressed view still stands:

Which structures and relationships best deliver the goods and services to the public?

Denationalization, deregulation and franchising are making inroads into a widening sector of the UK economy. These are one aspect of the general concept of **supply-side reform**, measures designed as micro-economic interventionism to raise productivity (dealt with in a companion volume in this series).

The Thatcher governments have put a juggernaut into motion which has attracted worldwide interest. Already two natural monopolies – gas and telephones – have been moved to the private sector. More – electricity and water – are to follow.

When a nationalized industry is denationalized, the relevant minister, whose departmental responsibility it is, launches the flotation publicity with suitably anodyne rhetoric which purports to be guaranteeing economic gains. The following is typical. The Secretary of State for the Environment announced the proposed privatization of the water authorities of England and Wales with:

'Their privatization will bring benefits to the customers, to the industry and to the nation in improved quality, more efficient service, greater commitment of the staff and more awareness of customer preference.'

This sounds constructive and positive, an exemplar of A-level textbook theory. The reality is much messier. Economists, were they somewhat more modest, would cease to quote with uncritical approval the famous, supportive words of J. M. Keynes:

'... the ideas of economists ... both when they are right and when they are wrong, are more powerful than is commonly understood. Indeed, the world is ruled by little else.'

Applied to the privatization programme since 1979, this claim looks less than convincing. The difference between economic theory and privatization reality for electricity, for example, announced earlier this year (1988) leaves a large credibility gap. The industry is to be broken into two sectors. The bigger part will include all the nuclear generating stations to make these as attractive as possible for the stock market. Simple economic theory suggests that a free market solution would not support nuclear power generation – even ignoring the Chernobyl factor – because such electricity is high-cost. A free market solution would produce cheaper electricity from coal-fired power stations.

The politicians who are the policy-makers adopt operational strategies which are the outcome of prejudice, pressure from interest groups, opportunism and ambition. In March 1988 the newspapers were full of the government's acceptance of the private flotation bid from British Aerospace for the Rover Group, for £150 million. It was not just the sophisticated analysts in the City who were astounded. A horizontal merger of the car group with another car manufacturer makes industrial sense, but when this was offered by Ford, two years earlier, the government, in a fit of xenophobia, turned it down; only a British suitor would be acceptable. As the government has to pay off £800 million worth of Rover Group debts for the deal to go through, this amounts to a dowry of £650 million paid by the government. It is one thing to sell the family silver, but to pay a dealer to take it away ...! The Secretary of State for Trade and Industry called it 'the deal of the decade'. Yes indeed.

Meanwhile, in economics, we take ourselves seriously and continue to approve of 'rational optimization', of 'allocative and productive efficiency' and the search for Paretian improvements in resource allocation. In the real world it is the politicians who are the 'practical men' (Keynes's now, rather dated, phrase), who have rolled back the frontier of the public sector and restructured the industrial landscape. What they have created needs a pragmatic evaluation of each privatization case to see if it yields aggregate net benefits that can justify it.

If only we could agree on how to measure aggregate net benefits! If I turn to an academic journal (*Fiscal Studies*) to check the gains or losses of the franchising of local authority services, I read that the cost savings are in the region of 20 per cent. This looks convincing, a supportive fact to include in this book. No sooner have I decided on this than the next issue of the same journal carries a refutation by another group of academics, who proceed to demolish the basis of the first article and then call into question the reliability of the figures which looked so convincing.

The virtues and defects of privatization are, indeed, to be found in the eye of the beholder.

```
                        KEY WORDS
    New Enlightenment        Medium-term financial strategy
    Job creation             Crowding out
    Investment appraisal     Sterling
    Buy-outs                 Balance of payments
    Competition policy       Invisibles account
    Fiscal policy            Spot price
    PSBR                     Supply-side reform
    Funding
```

Reading list

Sir Gordon Borrie, 'Competition, mergers and price fixing' in *Lloyds Bank Review*, April 1987.

Foreman and Peck, 'Natural monopoly and telecommunications, *Economic Review*, vol. 4, Sept. 1986.

Graham and Clarke, *The New Enlightenment*, Macmillan, 1986.

Harrison, *British Economy Survey*, vol. 16, no. 2, Spring 1987, pp. 41–44.

Hartley, 'An alternative explanation of public policies' in *Problems of Economic Policy*, Allen & Unwin, 1977.

Helm and Thompson, 'British Gas – the regulation of privatized monopolies', *Economic Review*, vol. 4, March 1987.

Molyneux and Thompson, 'Nationalized industries' performance: still third rate?', *Fiscal Studies*, Feb. 1987.

Thompson, 'Economics of privatization', *Economic Review*, vol. 3, Jan. 1986.

Essay topics

1. 'Selling off the family silver is a form of prodigality which merely subsidizes a riotous living: the country gets poorer.' Is this a valid criticism of privatization?
2. 'Privatization is the most important of the supply-side reforms of the 1980s.' Evaluate this claim.
3. 'With privatization the state gets a raw deal; it gets the bad industries; the private sector gets the good.' Evaluate this claim.
4. 'The virtues and defects of privatization are to be found in the eye of the beholder.' Discuss.

5. 'The privatization programme of the 1980s has not been based on aggregate net benefit but aggregate net financial gain to the Exchequer.' Evaluate this claim.
6. Will privatization make Britain more efficient?
7. What are the declared aims of the government's privatization plan, and is it achieving these in the programme achieved so far?
8. Would privatization of the NHS increase productive and allocative efficiency? State your case.
9. 'The government should not own and run any business' (Lord King, Chairman of newly privatized British Airways). Do you agree?
10. 'Competition policy and deregulation have now become the most important activity in tackling unemployment' (Lord Young, Secretary of State for Trade and Industry). Is this view tenable?

Data response question 6
Investing in water

Read the accompanying article taken from *The Times* of 13 July 1987. Then answer the following questions.
1. It would be normal to expect a 'red light' for moving a monopoly utility into the private sector because it does not have to compete for custom, yet the writer offers reassurance that 'pride and ambition' are the safety factors to protect the consumer. Are you convinced? Give your reasons.
2. What does the public gain if a privatized monopoly competes for finance?
3. Define regulation.
4. Why is the Treasury the worst monopolist of all?
5. Why are the benefits of floating the water industry less clear-cut than any previous major privatization. Explain in detail.
6. What is a quango?
7. What is the current way of assessing the cost of water consumption for a household? Why would an economist be critical of this method?
8. The 'RPI minus x' formula for pricing, as used for BT and BGC, would be inappropriate. Why?
9. Is water supply a perfectly reasonable subject for private provision?

Investing in water

The government no longer needs any ideological justification for privatizing companies that have to compete for business. The benefits are plain for all to see, across a wide range of former state concerns. The industrial and commercial case for moving monopoly utilities into the private sector is more subtle and still not universally accepted. It is nonetheless substantial.

Privatized monopolies might not have to compete for custom; they do have to compete for finance. And that is transmitted into better performance and efficiency by a variety of incentives (and emotions of pride and ambition) through management and employees who have a direct stake in profits.

In practice, regulation through an independent agency monitoring a formal operating licence provides better protection for the consumer than the theoretical accountability of public ownership. Moreover, a cash-hungry Treasury has often proved the worst monopolist.

Indeed, that was the spark for the planned privatization of the water industry. Mr Roy Watts, chairman of the profitable Thames Water Authority, fiercely resisted instructions to raise charges to customers unnecessarily, principally to cut government borrowing. He pointed to privatization as a preferable alternative for the consumer and for financing much-needed investment. When Whitehall realized that a sale of water authorities might be worth £10 billion, the idea was taken up with a sense of urgency bordering on haste.

The simple enthusiasm of those early days has been progressively blunted by the complex and detailed issues involved. Just a year ago, Mr Nicholas Ridley, the Environment Secretary, astutely abandoned the White Paper proposals made five months earlier by his predecessor Mr Kenneth Baker. Mr Ridley will shortly issue his new consultative document to pave the way for privatization. It will need to be skilfully judged, since the benefits of floating the water industry now seem less clearcut than in any previous major privatization.

The biggest difference is that the process of privatization is likely to involve a significant loss in efficient and effective water management to set against the benefits. Mr Baker's White Paper envisaged converting the integrated water authorities set up under the 1973 Water Act into public companies to be floated on the Stock Exchange. But widespread objections soon made it clear that this was too simplistic.

The authorities combined not only water supply and sewerage, but the integrated management of river basin systems, involving regulation of industrial discharges, pollution control, fisheries and wildlife protection. They also had a variety of related functions, including control of land drainage, flood prevention and sea defence duties and, in some cases such as the non-tidal Thames, control of river navigation.

Such basic public responsibilities, let alone policing the activities of anyone from manufacturers to anglers, could scarcely be vested in conventional shareholder-controlled companies. Yet the reorganization of water and sewerage to achieve integrated water management has been hailed as great a success as the contemporaneous reorganization of local government and health proved failures.

Just before the election, Mr Ridley wrote to the Water Authorities Association outlining a new scheme in which only water supply and sewerage were to be privatized. The authorities' duties to regulate, protect and improve the rivers were to be handed to a new Whitehall quango, the National Rivers Authority.

There are other problems. The National Rivers Authority has to be paid for, and the privatized authorities also have to charge their customers. General household metering lies many years ahead, and in the meantime, private companies will depend either on the rating system discredited for local government finance or be linked to the controversial planned community charge.

There is, in any case, no simple formula to exercise the control of prices of the kind that has rightly been judged essential when other monopoly utilities have been privatized. The costs of water and sewerage depend much more on financial charges such as interest on investment, which vary according to regional needs.

Breaking the links between operation, regulation and public finance carries the potentially important benefit of removing the incentive to shirk necessary improvements. That is something Mr Ridley should emphasize. According to City financial analysis, extra investment would also require price rises above the rate of inflation. This would no doubt be blamed on privatization, rather than recent Treasury parsimony, which has left Britain behind the rapid improvement in European Community standards of pollution and purity.

Converting water authorities into conventional companies will also remove any justification for the severe restrictions on the essentially non-profit statutory water companies, which provide a quarter of the water in England and Wales on behalf of the authorities. Astute industrialists are already investing in such companies in the expectation of higher returns on investment, which might again involve price increases blamed entirely on privatization.

Water supply is a perfectly reasonable subject for private provision. Private companies are likely to prove more efficient and cost-conscious operators in water and sewerage as in other activities. But if Mr Ridley is to overcome scepticism across the political spectrum, he will need to convince the public that removing the water industry from the financial constraints of the public sector will bring pure water from the taps and less pollution in rivers and on beaches – if not smaller bills.

Index